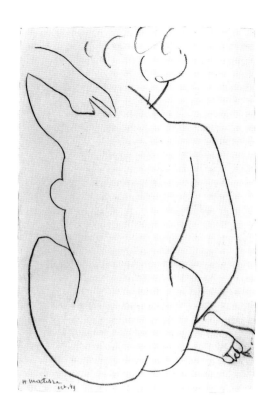

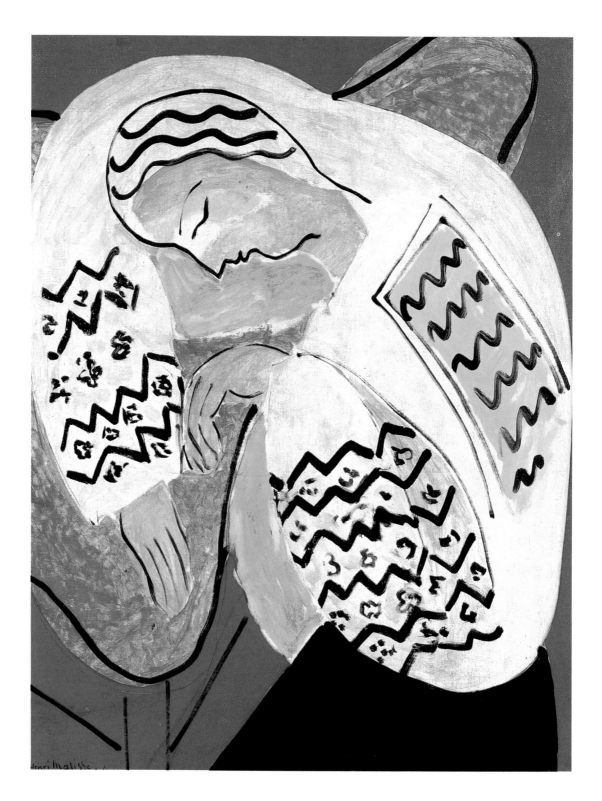

Volkmar Essers

HENRI MATISSE

1869–1954

Master of Colour

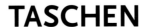

TASCHEN

KÖLN LONDON MADRID NEW YORK PARIS TOKYO

© 2002 TASCHEN GmbH
Hohenzollernring 53, D–50672 Köln
www.taschen.com
© 1989 Estate of Henri Matisse, Paris,
& VG Bild-Kunst, Bonn, for the reproductions
Edited and produced by Ingo F. Walther, Alling; Gilles Néret, Paris
Cover design: Catinka Keul, Angelika Taschen, Cologne

Printed in Germany
ISBN 3–8228–5977–X

Contents

6
In Quest of Pure Colour
1869-1905

18
Realism and Decoration
1906-1916

50
The Intimacy of the Nice Period
1917-1929

66
Beyond Spatial Limits
1930-1940

78
Matisse's Second Life: an Art of Grace
1941-1954

92
Henri Matisse 1869-1954:
A Chronology

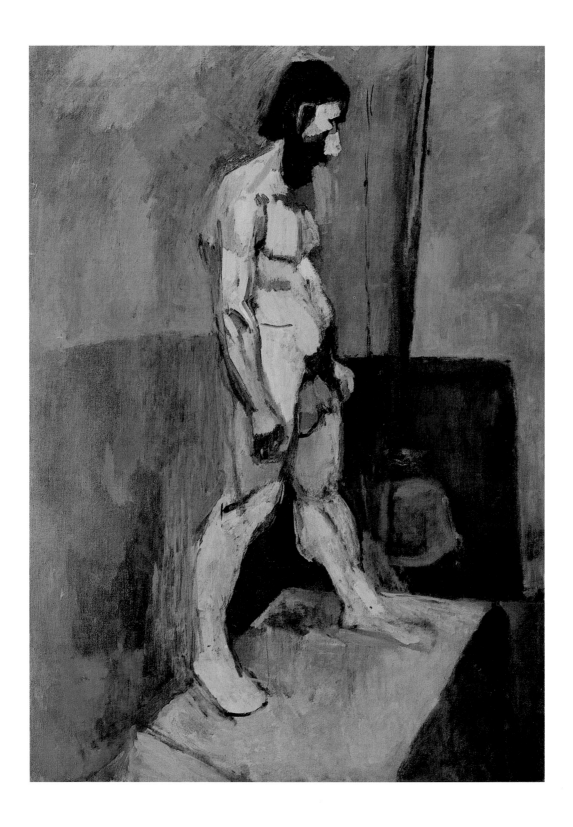

In Quest of Pure Colour
1869-1905

Destiny did not intend Henri Matisse to be a painter. He tells us himself that he was "the son of a seed merchant, due to take over the business from my father". Matisse was no precocious talent, no child prodigy like Pablo Picasso. Far more, the development of his life's work grew gradually and steadily out of an unparalleled devotion to colour, light and space, and the creation of harmony.

Matisse was born on 31st December 1869 at Le Cateau-Cambrésis in north-east France. His father, Emile Matisse, and his mother Héloise (née Gérard), both came from Le Cateau but were living in Bohain, where they kept a kind of household provisions store, with one extra department for seed and another for paint. Emile Matisse ruled with an iron paternal authority, and it was taken for granted that one day his son would follow in father's footsteps. But young Henri's health was poor and put paid to these plans.

The boy went to the Henri Martin grammar school in Saint Quentin (1882 – 1887), studied law for two years in Paris, toyed with the notion of becoming an apothecary, and in 1889 took work as a lawyer's assistant in Saint Quentin. And then, quite unexpectedly, he discovered his vocation as a painter. Through most of 1890 Matisse was confined to his bed with appendicitis; his mother gave him a box of paints to while away the time, and the young man discovered a passion. It was a passion that must surely have been latent already, for during his spell in the lawyer's office Matisse had been attending a course in drawing at the Quentin de la Tour foundation: the course was meant for curtain designers and was held in the top floor of the Palais de Fervaques from seven to eight o'clock in the morning.

Matisse quickly decided on painting and in 1890 or early 1891 returned to Paris in order to take William Bougereau's classes at the Académie Julian and prepare for the Ecole des Beaux-Arts entrance examinations. Bougereau nominated his pupil in January 1892; but Matisse failed the examination. Not long after his arrival in Paris,

Male Model, 1900
Oil on canvas, 99.3 x 72.7 cm
Museum of Modern Art, New York

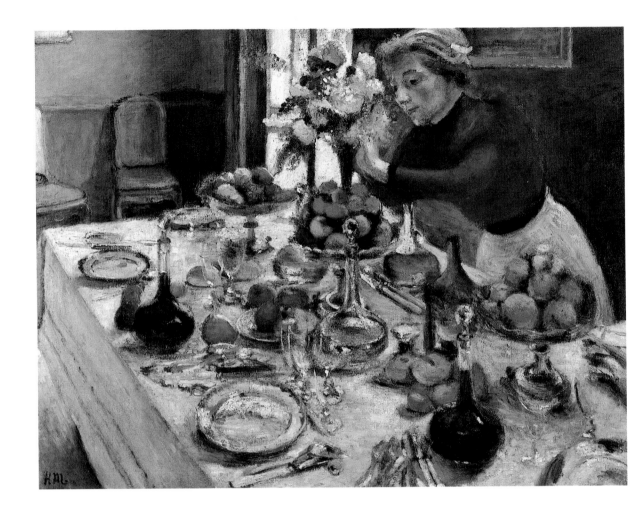

Dinner Table, 1897
Oil on canvas, 100 x 131 cm
Stavros S. Niarchos Collection

Right:
Studio under the Eaves, 1903
Oil on canvas, 55.2 x 46 cm
Fitzwilliam Museum, Cambridge

Matisse also attended the Ecole des Arts décoratifs, where he formed a long-lasting friendship with Albert Marquet. In March 1895, both Matisse and Marquet – after finally passing the exams – officially matriculated at the Ecole des Beaux-Arts as pupils of the Symbolist painter Gustave Moreau. They had already been regular visitors to Moreau's studio in 1893.

One of Matisse's neighbours at 19, Quai Saint-Michel was the painter Emile Wéry; with Wéry, Matisse travelled to Britanny in the summer of 1895, and through Wéry he first discovered Impressionism. On his return from Britanny, Matisse was filled with enthusiasm for prismatic colours, the colours of the rainbow, and his painting 'Dinner Table' (above) shows Matisse busy applying this new enthusiasm. In its controlled Impressionistic approach, the painting recalls Camille Pissarro, but it also shows Matisse's new quest for pure colour.

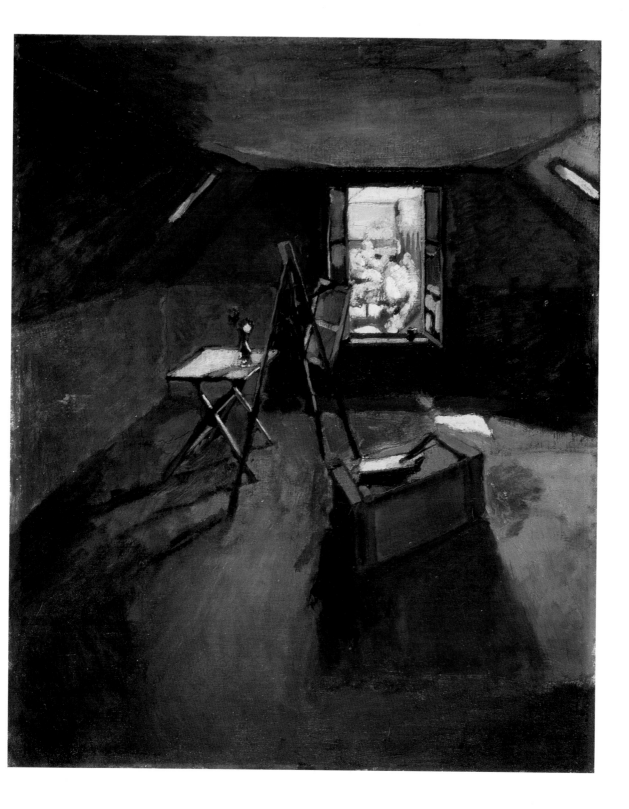

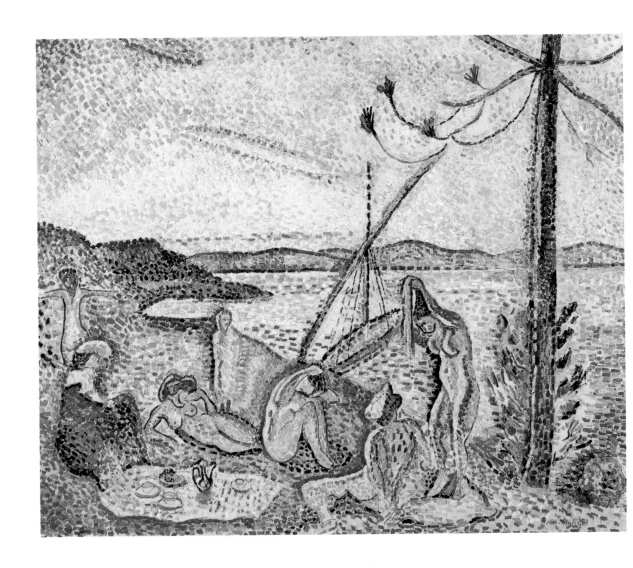

Luxe, calme et volupté, 1904
Oil on canvas, 98.3 x 118.5 cm
Musée National d'Art Moderne,
Centre Georges Pompidou, Paris

The young artist's growing interest in Impressionism was certain to vex the Symbolist Moreau. Yet mutual respect remained intact: Moreau valued his student highly, and in any case interiors, portraits, still lifes and landscapes remained subject to the valeurs system. In 1897, when 'Dinner Table' was exhibited at the Salon de la Nationale, Moreau was the first to defend Matisse against his opponents.

The following year Matisse quit the Ecole des Beaux-Arts, and exhibited at the Salon de la Nationale for the last time. Some years before he had got to know Amélie-Noémie-Alexandrine Parayre of Toulouse, in 1894 they had had a daughter, Marguerite, and now in 1898 they married. On Pissarro's advice, Matisse travelled to London

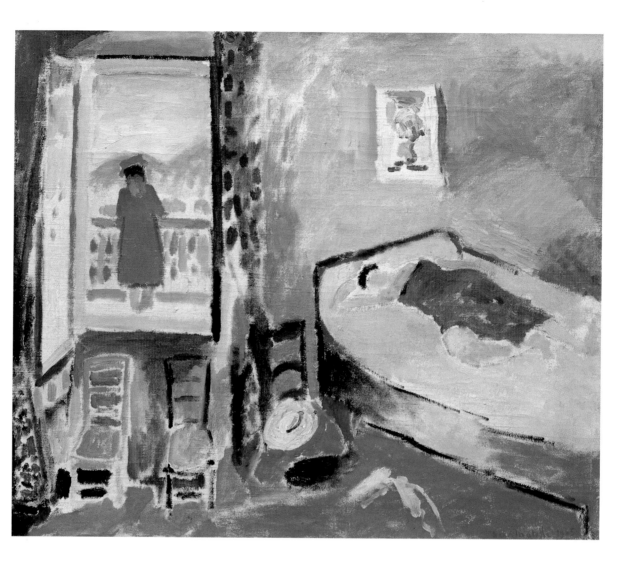

Interior at Collioure, 1905
Oil on canvas, 59 x 72 cm
Private collection, Switzerland

to see the paintings of J. M. W. Turner, taking his wife with him. After this honeymoon he returned to Paris, only to move on to Corsica, where he spent spring and summer in Ajaccio. This stay awakened his love of the south, and he painted a number of landscapes, still lifes and interiors, most of them on a small scale. The Mediterranean light invested his colours with a new brightness. That autumn Matisse and his wife moved to Toulouse, and their first son, Jean, was born in nearby Fenouillet, to be followed in 1900 by a second son, Pierre, born at Bohain.

The Matisse family now returned to Paris, to 19, Quai Saint-Michel. The years ahead were often difficult: Matisse painted, his wife ran a milliner's shop, and the children were often left in their

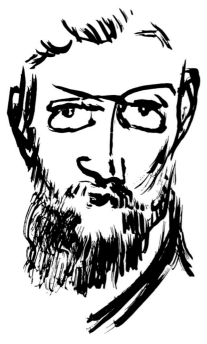

Self-Portrait, 1900
Brush and ink

grandparents' care. When Matisse returned to the Ecole des Beaux-Arts, Fernand Cormon, the successor to Gustave Moreau (who had died in 1889), demanded that Matisse leave the atelier, along with Marquet and Charles Camoin. Cormon pointed out that Matisse was over the age limit of thirty. At that stage, Matisse did not yet feel ready for full independence: he returned to the Académie Julian for a short period, and subsequently moved to another academy, newly founded by one Camillo, where the tutor was Eugène Carrière, a friend of the sculptor Auguste Rodin. Matisse got to know André Derain, and Derain introduced him to his friend Maurice de Vlaminck. And all the while Matisse was producing still lifes, views of Paris, nude studies, and sculptures.

Matisse spent a great deal of time in the museums, but also in avantgarde galleries such as Ambroise Vollard's, where in 1899 he bought a drawing by Van Gogh, Rodin's plaster bust of Henri de Rochefort, a painting by Paul Gauguin ('Young Man with Tiaré Flower'), and Paul Cézanne's 'Bathers'. From 1900 to 1904, Cézanne was a decisive influence on Matisse, as we can see in his 'Male Model' (p. 6). Male nudes are rare in Matisse; he produced them only in the period from 1899 to 1903, when he was at his most enthusiastic about Cézanne. Matisse made this note concerning his method: "I emphasize character, and do not flinch from the risk of forfeiting charm, since what I stand to gain is greater solidity." What reminds us most strongly of Cézanne in 'Male Model' is the position Matisse has opted for, tense rather than relaxed. The man stands firmly, legs apart. Grace or elegance are subordinate to colour, and the different planes clash and contrast.

Matisse and his wife could not make a living from the sale of paintings and hats, so Matisse began to accept demanding commissions. He and Marquet took on the task of decorating the Grand Palais in Paris for the Great Exhibition in 1900. It was exhausting work, and when it was finished he and his wife retreated to Bohain for a well-earned rest. Matisse was not in the best of health, and was so despondent that he considered giving up painting. 'Studio under the Eaves' (p. 9) gives an impression of his struggle for survival. It is a gloomy, dungeon-like painting, with little light or colour. The tree blossoming outside the open window is a promise of revelation, an image within the image. Matisse was later to tell his son Pierre: "That was the transition from valeurs to colours".

Matisse got over his despondency and began to look for collectors and opportunities to exhibit. He participated in a joint show at the Salon d'Automne (founded in 1903) and in 1904 had his first solo exhibition at Ambroise Vollard's gallery. In 1905 at the Salon des Indépendants he exhibited a painting done in 1904, 'Luxe, calme et volupté' (p. 10), which was promptly bought by Paul Signac. Matisse had got to know Signac one summer in St. Tropez, and had read his

André Derain, 1905
Oil on canvas, 39.5 x 29 cm
Tate Gallery, London

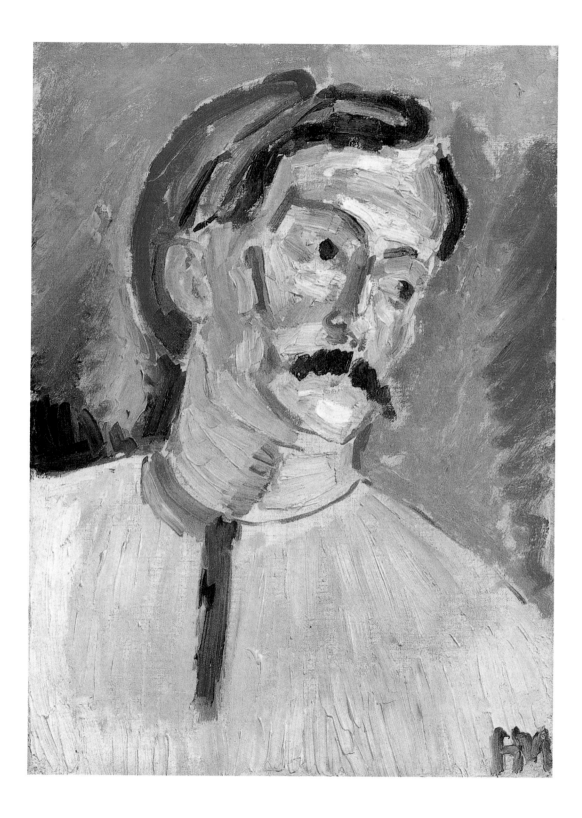

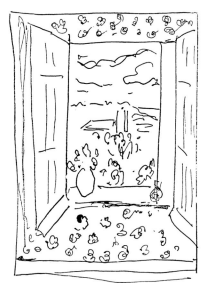

View from the Window at Collioure, 1905
Pen and ink
Private collection

book 'From Delacroix to Neo-Impressionism' as early as 1898 or 1899. Signac's method of analysing colour appealed to Matisse, and he adopted it as a means of modelling light through colour. For his conception he was indebted to Cézanne's 'Bathers', but his use of colour was an analytic separation into small planes. If Matisse had hoped that this mosaic approach would create a new unity of effect he was to be disappointed, and himself wrote: "Breaking up colour lead to the breaking-up of form and outline. What you are left with is an all-too-apparent surface, nothing but a tease of the retina that destroys the repose of surface and outline."

Matisse spent the summer of 1905 at Collioure, a fishing village on the Mediterranean, with André Derain and (at times) Maurice de Vlaminck. His 'Interior at Collioure' (p. 11) was painted that summer, as was the portrait of his friend and fellow-artist Derain (p. 13). The sojourn in Collioure represented an important turning-point in Matisse's creative life.

In 1905 Matisse, Derain, Vlaminck and Marquet exhibited jointly at the autumn salon in Paris, and immediately a storm of public controversy broke out. Their unrestrained colours led critic Louis Vauxcelles to dub them the Fauves ("wild ones"). The Fauves made colour the major element in their paintings, and were unanimous in their rejection of the nuances of the Impressionist palette and their quest for the expressive potential of pure colours. Realistic reflection of Nature played little part in their aims. Matisse was the main target of criticism, particularly his 'Woman with the Hat' (right), which he had completed barely in time for the show. It was the biggest of the pictures he submitted to the salon. Dressed in a costly gown and magnificent hat, like an elegant lady posing for a formal bourgeois portrait, Madame Matisse is three-quarters turned to the viewer. Conventional forms are replaced by lurid patches of colour. Her face is the least affected by the process, but still it is trapped between the explosive colours of the hat and dress. Michael Stein bought the painting. This succès de scandale saved Matisse from ruin and sent prices for his paintings soaring. Leo, Gertrude, Michael and Sarah Stein all bought numerous of his works, and urged others to do the same.

In 'Madame Matisse, "The Green Line"' (p. 16), another portrait of the painter's wife, the colours are still turbulent but the overall effect is tranquil. Nothing is dictated by chance in this presentation; Matisse has concentrated on the essentials. The majestic quality and front-facing position lend the portrait the charisma of an icon. And the green line, which at first glance seems unnatural and wilful, in fact marks a boundary between zones of light and shadow, and at the same time emphasizes the even features, indeed the beauty, of this face. Of course the line also signals the division of the painting into areas of colour that are mutually complementary and in no way

Woman with the Hat, 1905
Oil on canvas, 81 x 65 cm
Private collection, San Francisco

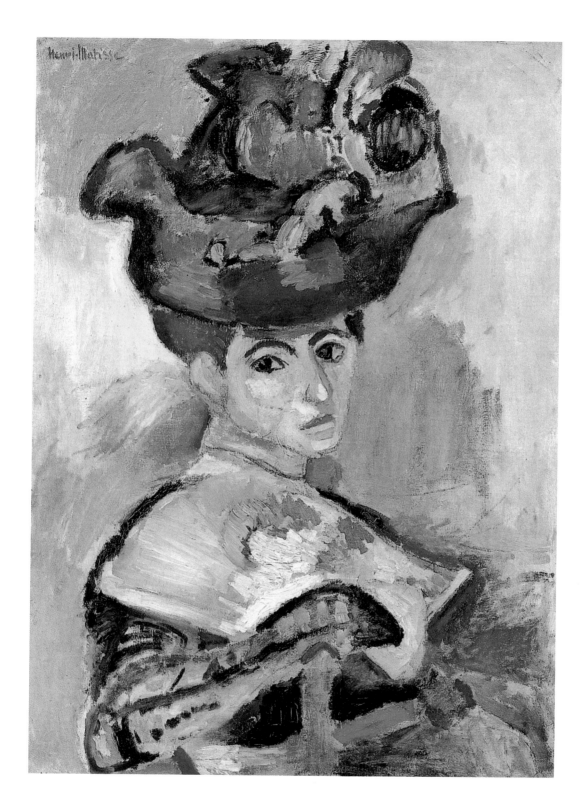

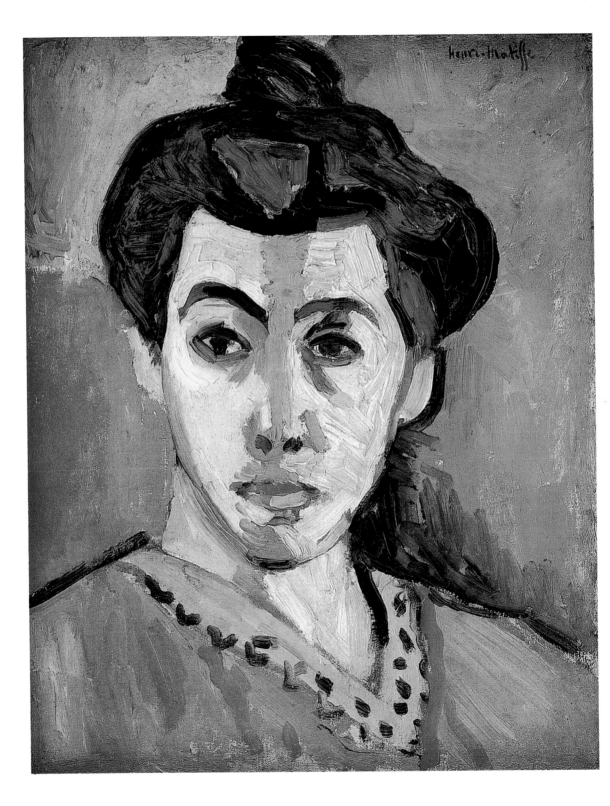

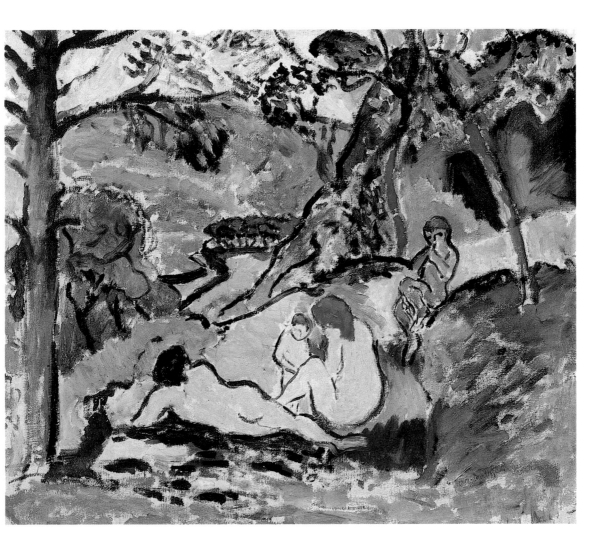

devalued by the division. What concerned Matisse was not so much painting his wife's portrait as creating an image, and for Matisse "painting an image" meant a construction in colour.

As well as richly contrastive zones of colour, Matisse repeatedly used rhythmic lines and ornamentation. In his 'Pastoral' (above) Matisse re-used the motif of 'Luxe, calme et volupté' and at the same time established his theme of joie de vivre and the golden age. These were to be the main constituents in his life's work.

Pastoral, 1905
Oil on canvas, 46 x 55 cm
Musée d'Art Moderne de la Ville de Paris, Paris

LEFT:
Madame Matisse, "The Green Line", 1905
Oil on canvas, 40.5 x 32.5 cm
Statens Museum for Kunst, Copenhagen

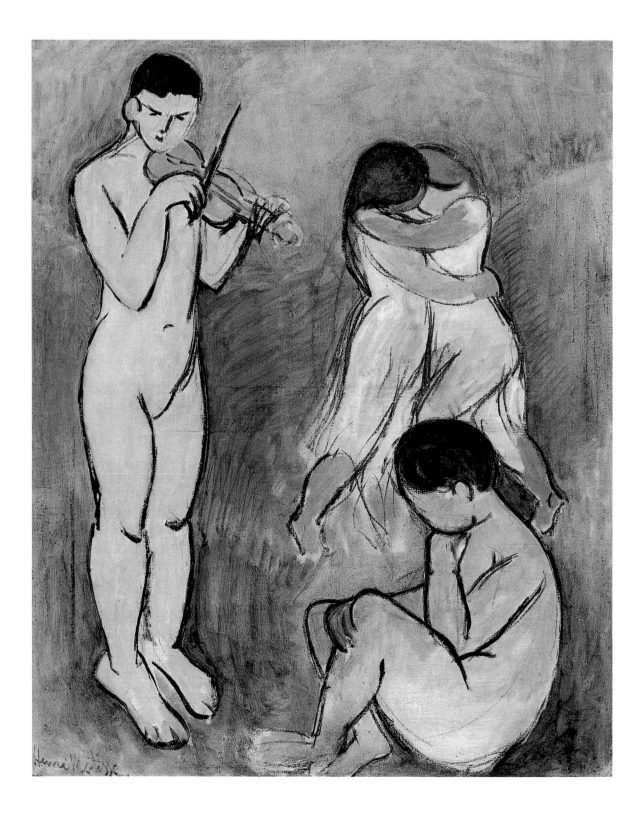

Realism and Decoration
1906-1916

In his own opinion, Matisse's life's work began with the painting 'La Joie de vivre' (p. 20). It was the only work he exhibited at the 1906 Salon des Indépendants, and again Matisse provoked violent controversy. Signac, for instance, felt that the lines around the zones of colour amounted to treason: "Up till now I have valued Matisse, but he seems to have taken the wrong direction. Across a painting two and a half metres broad he has framed his odd figures in lines the thickness of your thumb. Then he has smothered the lot in lacklustre, clearly marked-off colours which may well be pure but are still revolting. Ah, these pastel pinks! It is all reminiscent of the worst of Ranson (in the 'Nabi' period), or dear old Anquetin's most despicable cloisonism – or the garish shop-signs at the ironmonger's or haberdasher's." For Leo Stein, the painting was the most important in modern times, and he bought it. In Gertrude and Leo Stein's home it could be seen by all who valued the avantgarde, among them Picasso, a regular visitor. The two artists gave each other their paintings and achieved a mutual if distant admiration. Matisse showed Picasso an African mask he had bought. When in 1907 'La Joie de vivre' lost pride of place in the Stein house it was to Picasso's 'Demoiselles d'Avignon' (Museum of Modern Art, New York), the painting which inaugurated Cubism. Wassily Kandinsky, in his book 'Concerning the Spiritual in Art' (1912) in which he expounded a theory of abstract art, took the contrast between the two painters as exemplary: "Matisse – colour. Picasso – form. Two approaches to one great goal." Leo Stein, on the other hand, took sides: he sold Matisse's masterpiece to the American Albert Barnes, who hung it in his remote hideaway at Merion, where only a very few could see it.

This painting with the literary title, 'La Joie de vivre', had been prepared by Matisse with great care, to ensure a high degree of clarity and harmony. The stronger colours – green, orange, violet, blue, pink, yellow – occupy the spaces that the trees, figures and landscapes

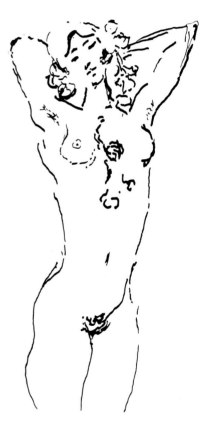

Female Nude. Study for
'La Joie de Vivre', 1905
Pen and ink

LEFT:
Music (Sketch), 1907
Oil on canvas, 73.4 x 60.8 cm
Museum of Modern Art, New York

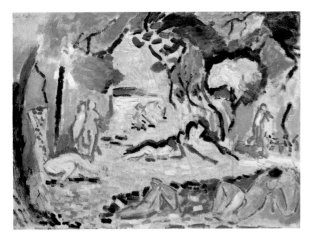 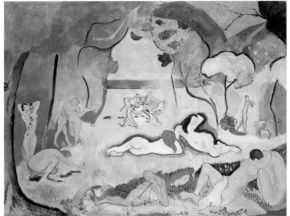

ABOVE LEFT:
Sketch for 'La Joie de Vivre', 1905
Oil on canvas, 41.2 x 55 cm
Haas Collection, San Francisco

ABOVE RIGHT:
La Joie de Vivre, 1905/6
Oil on canvas, 174 x 238 cm
Barnes Foundation, Merion (Pa.)

"In this picture, for the first time, Matisse deliberately achieves his intention of drawing the lines of the human body so as to harmonize the visual values of unmixed colours to which nothing has been added but white – to harmonize, and to simplify. He puts his systematic twists of draughtmanship to the same use as you would put discord in music, or vinegar or lemon in cooking – the way you would use eggshells to fine coffee."   GERTRUDE STEIN

naturally dictate. The figures themselves are at once symbolic and ornamental, in the pastoral tradition of bacchanals and nymphs. A bucolic atmosphere of Daphne and Chloe prevails. It is a Golden Age an age in which Man and Nature are at one.

In the oil sketch 'Music' (p. 18) Matisse pursues his theme of dance and music. In style it is a spontaneous painting, not sufficiently advanced beyond its realistic starting-point. The figures are forcefull defined, and are positioned in a setting free of all other detail. In calling the work a sketch, Matisse was announcing his intention of reworking it at a later date.

In May 1906 Matisse travelled from Perpignan to Algeria, where he visited the oasis of Biskra. For the space of the two-week journey he did not paint: "One is quite aware that it would be necessary to spend years in such countries to find anything new, and that one cannot simply come along and apply one's own palette and method." It was not until after his return to Collioure that he painted the 'Blue Nude' (right), subtitled 'Souvenir of Biskra'. The palms in the background are the only indication of locality; the nude herself has evolved from the reclining figure in 'Luxe, calme et volupté' and 'La Joie de vivre'. The nude was to occupy a major position in Matisse's painting in due course; meanwhile he tried approaching the same position in a different medium, in his sculpture 'Reclining Nude'.

The themes of Matisse's sculptural work developed parallel to his painting. In this case, the sculpture accidentally fell to the floor. Mercifully it was possible to save it. "In the meantime I took a large canvas and painted the 'Souvenir of Biskra'," recalled Matisse. Without any alteration, the shape and position of the clay figure were put into the painting, complete with its twists and awkwardness. In the process it came to seem particularly large, dynamic and powerfu

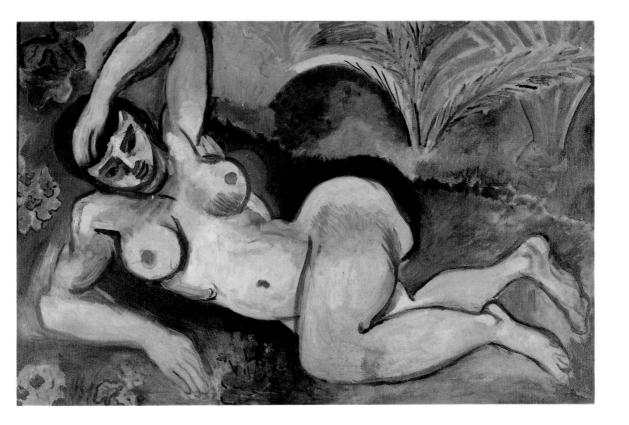

The female body reclines heavily, casting a shadow. The impact of the painting is determined by the tension between this woman's physical presence and the spatial flatness of the setting. Matisse held as a maxim that the human figure should be dominant: "What interests me most is the figure, not some still life or landscape. Painting the human figure is the best way for me to express what I might call my own peculiar religious feeling about life."

Matisse returned from Biskra with ceramics, cloths, and other objects that he frequently found a use for in his paintings. What changed his image of the East, far more than the general impressions of his travels, were the arts and crafts he had seen, and Islamic art became a crucial point of reference for him. The Musée des Arts décoratifs in Paris had mounted exhibitions of Islamic art in 1893, 1894, and most importantly 1903, and the Louvre's extensive Islamic collection could be viewed at any time. Rather less of a museum atmosphere prevailed at the Great Exhibition in 1900, at the Turkish, Persian, Moroccan, Tunisian, Algerian, and Egyptian pavilions. Islamic ceramics gave Matisse rules of thumb that were vital in his

Blue Nude
(Souvenir of Biskra), 1906
Oil on canvas, 92 x 140 cm
Baltimore Museum of Art, Baltimore

"I am unable to make any distinction between the feeling I get from life and the way I translate that feeling into painting." HENRI MATISSE

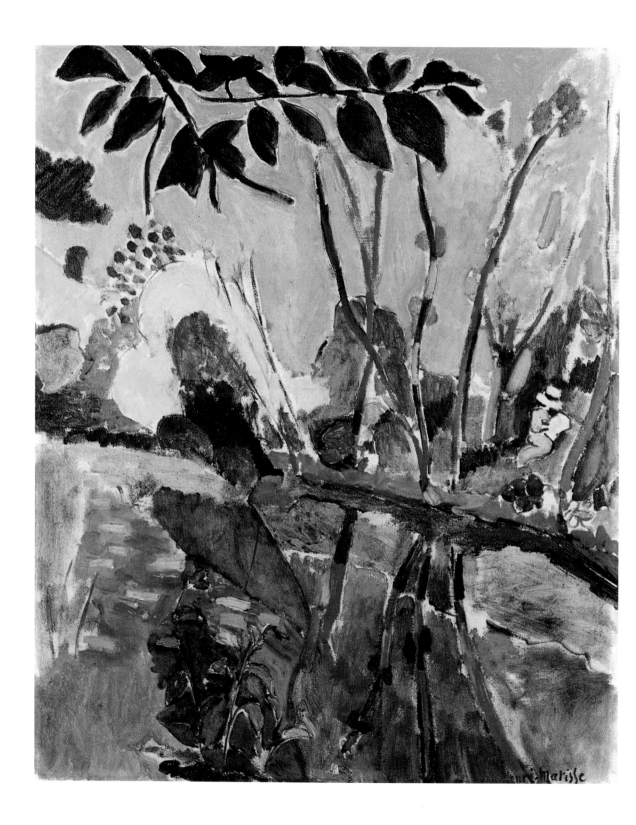

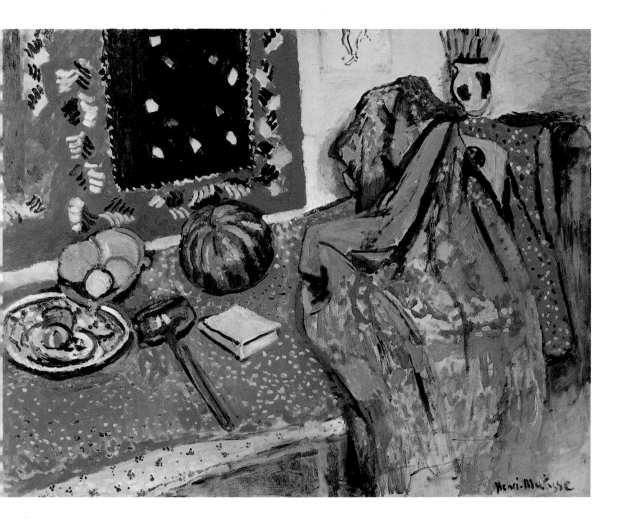

own work: colours were applied pure and in flat planes, draughts-manship was reduced to arabesque lines, and dimensional space was rendered flatly. All manner of surfeit and luxury were permitted as long as they were lightly and decoratively used. The aim was to achieve a maximum of splendour with a minimum of effort: to do this, Matisse came to prefer a tendril-like arabesque ornamentation.

Not only ceramics gave Matisse his access to the Orient: carpets were important too, and surely no other modern painter can have allotted so central a role in his work to carpets and cloths. 'Oriental Rugs' (above) signals the beginning of Matisse's decorative art. The painting, though, is still burdened with conflict: the colours are weighty, the objects solid and tactile. The still life of fruits, longhandled pot, watermelon and book establishes spatial values that

Oriental Rugs, 1906
Oil on canvas, 89 x 116.5 cm
Musée de Peinture et de Sculpture, Grenoble

LEFT:
The Bank, 1907
Oil on canvas, 73 x 60.5 cm
Kunstmuseum, Basle

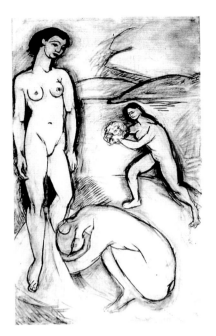

Study for 'Luxe I', 1907
Charcoal, 277 x 137 cm
Musée National d'Art Moderne,
Centre Georges Pompidou, Paris

"Music and colour doubtless have no more nor less in common than that they travel the same direction. Seven notes, with the slightest of variations, are enough to call for the most glorious of creations. Why should it be otherwise in the visual arts?"
HENRI MATISSE

Luxe I, 1907
Oil on canvas, 210 x 138 cm
Musée National d'Art Moderne,
Centre Georges Pompidou, Paris

are at odds with the flat dimensions of decorativeness. And the diagonals in the cloths clearly preserve a sense of depth, especially the deep folds in the green material in the foreground. Oriental flatness and realistic depth are at variance in the painting.

Decoration, for Matisse, was a means of expressing the spirit through pure colours, abstract arabesques, flat dimensions, and rhythm. Decorative art does not show its spiritual content: it requires us to infer it. Matisse learnt this from Islamic art. But in considering occidental art, whether the draughtmanship or the colour was the prime value, he now looked with new eyes, and in 1907, after he had visited Florence, Arezzo, Siena and Padua in Italy, he noted: "When I behold Giotto's frescoes in Padua I may have difficulty working out which scene in Christ's life I am looking at, but I sense the feeling in it. The feeling is in the lines, the composition, the colour. All the title can do is confirm my impression."

As early as 1907 Matisse began to quote motifs from his own pictures, endowing them with a kind of monumental status. The three women bathers in 'Luxe I' (right) have been quoted from 'Luxe, calme et volupté'. But in their size they are plainly inspired by Puvis de Chavanne's 'Girls on the Sea Shore' (Louvre, Paris), which Matisse had seen in 1895 in the Salon de la Nationale. Puvis de Chavanne had breathed new life, and a kind of strict clarity, into the art of decorative mural painting. His work had excited Matisse's admiration; and the main figure in Matisse's painting has a majestic presence, like a Venus risen from the waves. Her less stately companions, though in drying or bearing a bouquet they are engaged in prosaic business, share a certain dignity, as if they were in the service of a goddess.

The southern landscape around Collioure continued to inspire Matisse. Now, in contrast to his Fauvist period, the bright light gave his colours an almost transparent quality, and foreground and background merged in the new distribution of colour. In 'The Bank' (p. 22) muted tones of violet, blue and green flatten the foreground while the warmer green and orange highlight the background. The lines of the bank and the path mark out the axis of image and reflection, and in the inverted repetition the landscape is transformed into the abstraction of a pattern.

Sarah Stein, together with the German painters Hans Purrmann and Oskar Moll, revered Matisse as a great master and urged him to found a school. This he did; and from 1907 to 1909 he taught and by the end had some sixty students. However, Matisse was very alert to any distractions from his own artistic work, and found himself forced to close the school: "By the time I had sixty students there were one or two among them that were promising. Monday to Saturday I sweated blood to make lions of these sheep. It demanded a great deal of energy, and I wondered what I really wanted to be, a professor or a painter? And so I closed the atelier down."

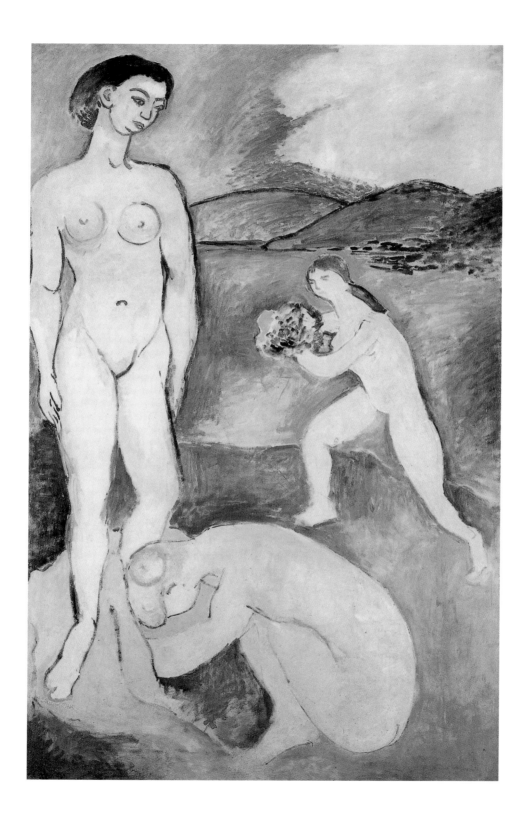

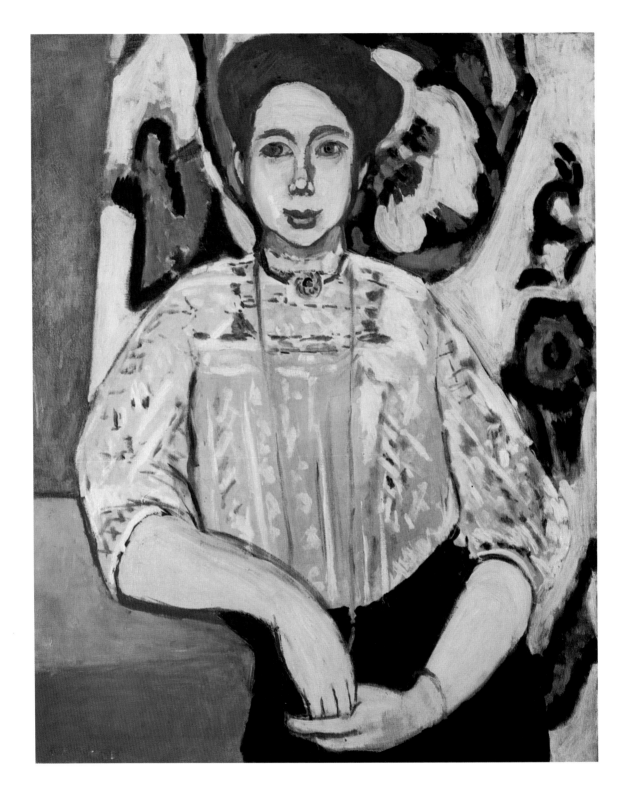

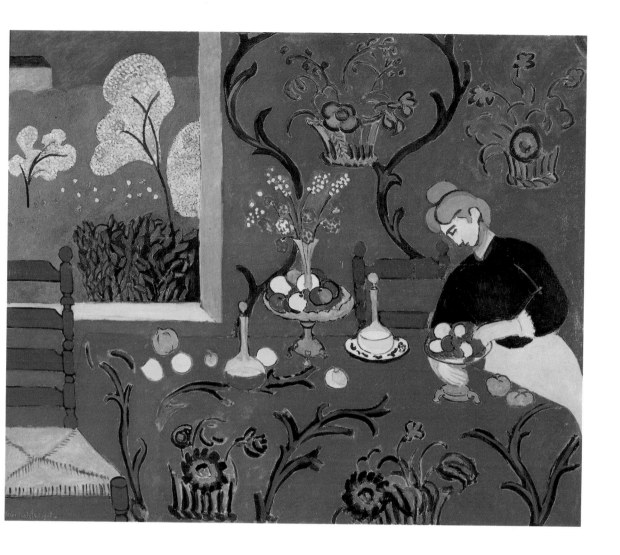

In 1908, with Purrmann, he made his first trip to Germany. Oskar Moll's wife Greta, who was one of Matisse's students, commissioned her portrait (left) in the same year. The painting progressed slowly, and it was not until he had refreshed his memory of a Paolo Veronese portrait in the Louvre that Matisse found his solution: he altered the shape and position of the arms and eyebrows, and gave a greater hardness to the forms. "And suddenly it has an amazing grandeur and splendour," observed Matisse, astonished. In portrait painting the closing of the gap between the realistic starting-point and the formal goal was most problematic of all. Greta Moll was not alone among

Harmony in Red, 1908
Oil on canvas, 180 x 200 cm
Hermitage, Leningrad

LEFT:
Greta Moll, 1908
Oil on canvas, 93 x 73.5 cm
National Gallery, London

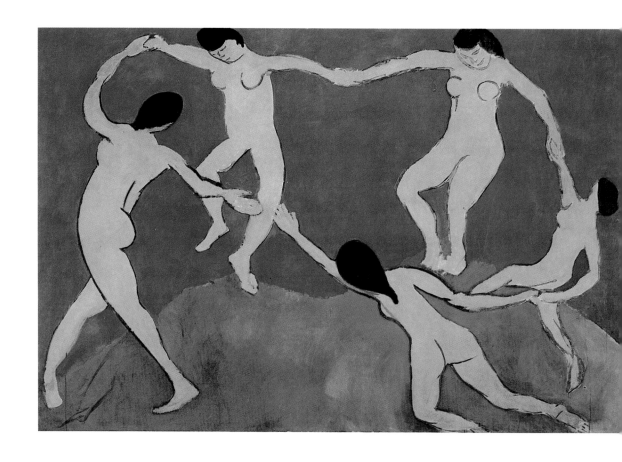

La Danse (first version), 1909
Oil on canvas, 259.7 x 390.1 cm
Museum of Modern Art, New York

Matisse's models in her disinclination to accept a portrait which the
artist had subjected entirely to his own formal conceptions.

Henri Matisse had by now achieved recognition and was a
well-to-do man. In 1909 he left the Quai Saint-Michel and bought a
house at Issy-les-Moulineaux, in the grounds of which he built the
studio where many of his major works were to be created. At last he
was able to set his father's mind at rest, and invited the anxious parent
to visit his new security: house, garden and pond, flower-beds,
spinney.

Sergei Shchukin, a Russian collector who had begun his Matisse
collection in 1908, bought a painting that was exhibited at the autumn
salon with the title 'Harmony in Blue' – a painting that had in fact
begun life as a harmony in green. To Shchukin's surprise, when the
painting was delivered in 1909 it had been metamorphosed into a
'Harmony in Red' (p. 27). Matisse had reworked it. In its green state,
there was too little contrast in the picture between the interior and the
springtime scene visible through the window. And blue was not

"One note is simply a colour. Two notes make
a chord, and life."   HENRI MATISSE

28

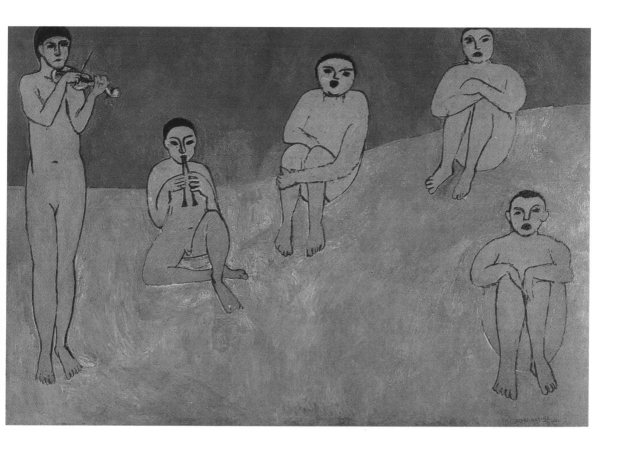

abstract enough, since it was the actual colour of the Jouy linen on the wall and table. Not till he used red did Matisse dispel all suggestion of naturalism. Although the painting conforms to the laws of perspective, the effect of the blue-patterned red cloth which covers both table and wall is to flatten the planes and dimensions. A view from a window had been a favourite artistic motif since the Renaissance, and recurs in many of Matisse's works throughout his career. Both the painting and the window are confined in the same rectangular shape, and in several of his works it is difficult at first to distinguish the two frames. The servant busy at the table seems almost to be engaged in some ceremonial ritual.

'Harmony in Red' shows Matisse recasting his painting of 1897, at that date still under Impressionist influence, in the decorative style. The subject remains the same. The servant girl, on the right in both paintings, is setting things straight on the table, presiding over crockery, caraffes, fruit and the main centrepiece of fruit and flowers. In 'Dinner Table' (1897) the luxuriously laid table seems to blend with

La Musique, 1910
Oil on canvas, 260 x 398 cm
Hermitage, Leningrad

PAGES 30/31:
La Danse, 1909/10
Oil on canvas, 260 x 391 cm
Hermitage, Leningrad

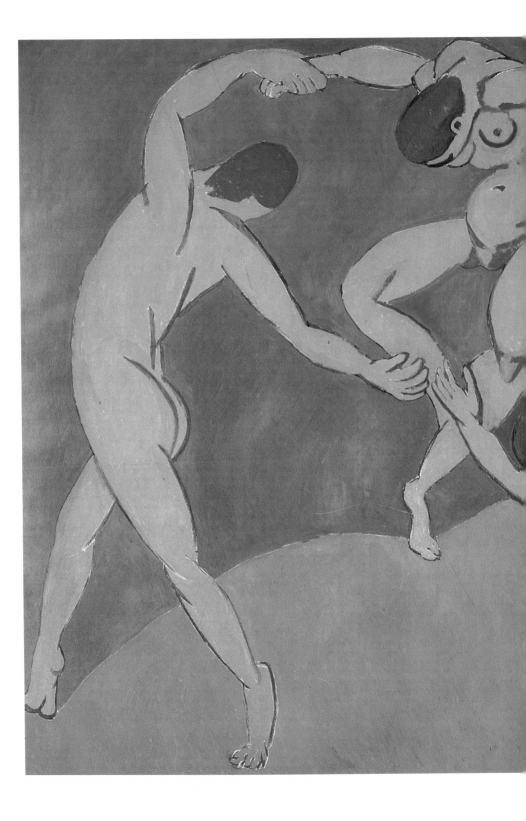

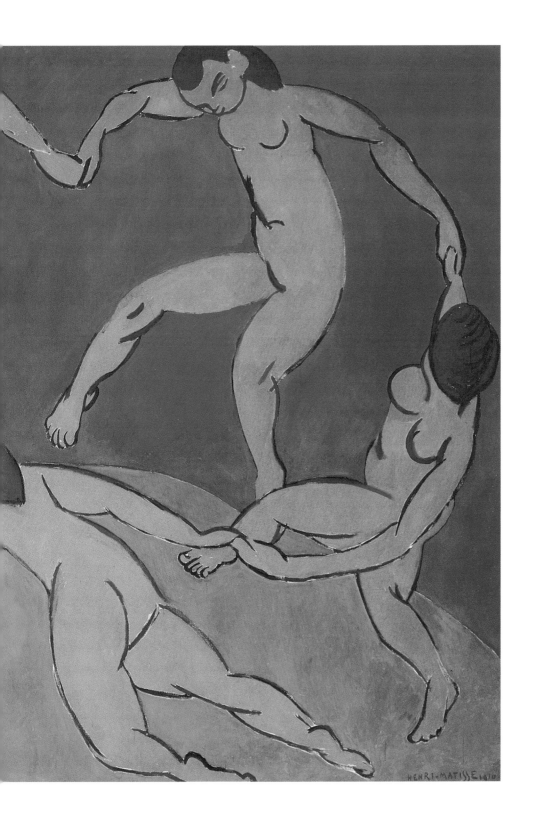

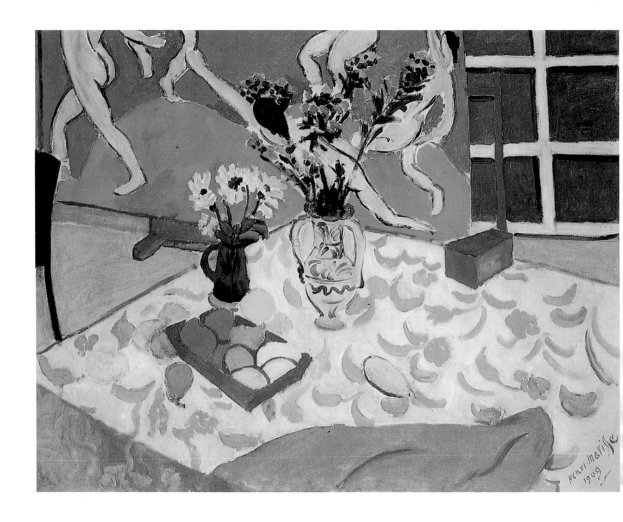

Still Life with 'La Danse', 1909
Oil on canvas, 89 x 116 cm
Hermitage, Leningrad

"What interests me most is not the still life
nor the landscape either. It is the human figure."
HENRI MATISSE

the depths of the room, and the servant is an agent of order and
domesticity. In 'Harmony in Red', by contrast, she is scarcely more
than a silhouette, and the movement of her hands and the position of
her head have been subordinated to the rhythmic patterning of wall
and tablecloth.

In 1909 Shchukin offered Matisse a further commission. He
ordered two large murals: 'La Danse' and 'La Musique'. The first
version of 'La Danse' had impressed Shchukin with a quality of
"noblesse". Both versions – the first, in the Museum of Modern Art in
New York (p. 28) and the final, in the Leningrad Hermitage (pp. 30/3
– have distinctive and different colour qualities: red versus pink,
ultramarine versus sky-blue, emerald green versus Veronese green.
The choice of colours in 'La Danse' and 'La Musique' has its

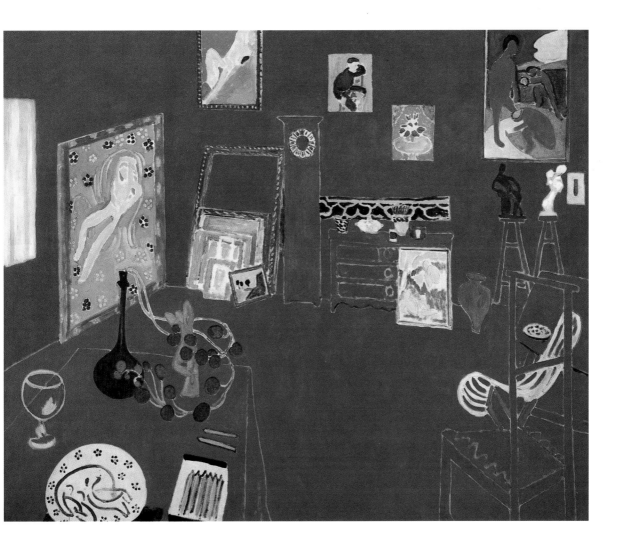

forerunner in Persian ceramics and miniatures which, until the 13th century, often used pure reds, greens and blues in creating ornamental surfaces.

'La Danse' shows Matisse quoting a motif from 'La Joie de Vivre' and giving it a new magnitude. His dancers link hands and form an energetic circle, or rather (the spatial perspective redefines the shape) an oval. Faster they dance, on the top of their hill. The right-hand bias of the oval suggests clockwise movement, and emphasizes the irregular energy of the dance. Between the figure on the far left and the dancer on its right there is a gap: the woman in the foreground is closing it, trying to complete the circle once more, by reaching for the

The Red Studio, 1911
Oil on canvas, 181 x 219 cm
Museum of Modern Art, New York

"A young painter who cannot liberate himself from the influence of past generations is digging his own grave."   HENRI MATISSE

hand the other dancer is stretching out – and her partner, in stretching out, is twisting, and slowing down the momentum that is bearing her on into the background. The contact is not quite achieved, and the viewer is left to close the gap himself. The energetic effort of the dance almost distorts the figures, but it is a distortion that complements their expressiveness.

A "religion of happiness" was made incarnate in 'La Danse'. For Matisse, the farandole, a round-dance popular in Provence, expressed the very essence of rhythm and joie de vivre. Decorative style and human figure harmonize in 'La Danse' and communicate a subtly infective sense of life and joy. As for the great dignity of the figures, it can largely be explained in formal terms: their monumentality and majesty derive from the simplification of the artistic strategy – a few big and homogeneous areas of colour, a tendency toward pure line drawing, a strong sense of outline.

'La Musique' (p. 29) deploys the same elements: five red bodies, a green hill, and a blue sky. The male figures in 'La Musique' are not linked by any unifying dynamic, such as the oval motif of 'La Danse'; instead, they are isolated, arranged in a row like musical notes. The flautist is related to his counterpart in the 'Pastoral', and the violinist has been retained from 'Music (Sketch)'. In the interim, though, they have changed their positions. Rather than being three-quarter turned, they now face the viewer frontally, and in so doing they are not only more emphatically separated from each other but also make a full-face demand for the viewer's attention.

In 'La Danse' Matisse had tried to extract the utmost in non-realistic spirituality from his decorative two-dimensionality. Now he felt the need to return to the realistic and everyday, and did so with 'Still Life with "La Danse"' (p. 32). 'La Danse' is included in a studio view, foreshortened and at an angle that leads into the diagonal of the table. A still life with a fruit dish, box and vases occupies the area where the table's diagonals most plainly signal the painting's spatiality.

Decorative and realistic phases were to alternate throughout Matisse's life. One work will be so nearly abstract as to exclude realistic spatiality; another will be informed by careful scrutiny of given reality, down to the last brushstroke. In this ambivalence we may see the unceasing dichotomy of oriental and occidental aesthetics in Matisse, or equally the split in the artist between the more Romantic and the more sobrely scientific sides of his temperament.

In 'The Red Studio' (p. 33) the crayons, easels, plinths, frames, paintings, sculptures and ceramics lie strewn on a monochrome surface like the pattern of a carpet. Whatever spatial properties the chair, table, clock, chest and other objects might have are dispelled by this use of a single colour. Pictures of his studio often spelt out

The Algerian Woman, 1909
Oil on canvas, 81 x 65 cm
Musée National d'Art Moderne,
Centre Georges Pompidou, Paris

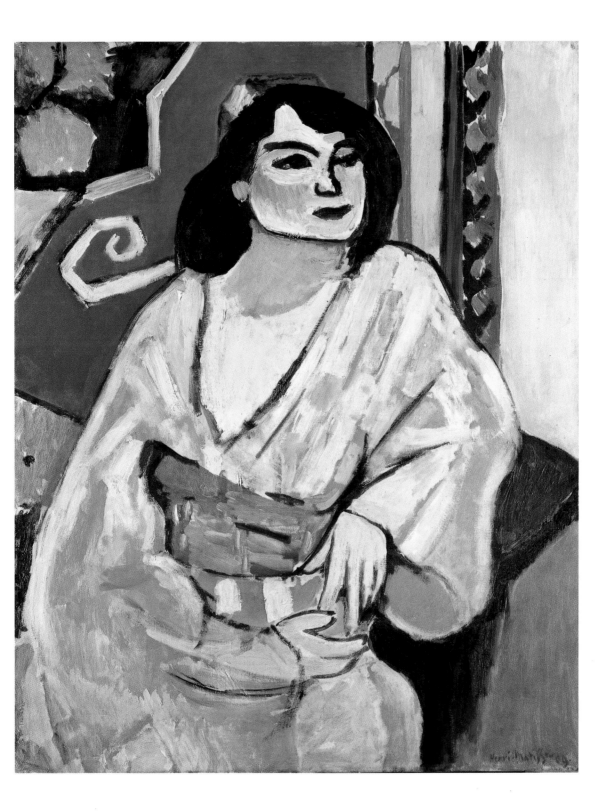

Matisse's programme and indeed his very self: "What really concern
me, above all else, is expression." In contrast to the intensified
emotionalism of the German Expressionists of the 'Brücke', Matisse
wanted painting to express itself, to be its own world. Repeatedly he
examined his own creative premises, and observed: "For me,
expression is not a question of some passion that might be visible in a
face or seen in some violent movement. It is located in the entirety of
my painting: the position the figures are in, the empty spaces around
them, the proportions – all of it contributes. The art of composition
consists in ordering various elements that are available to a painter for
the expression of his feelings in a pleasing manner. Every part must be
visible in a painting and must play its appropriate role, whether
principal or secondary. Anything that is not necessary to the painting
damages it. A work must establish an overall harmony: any
superfluous detail will drive out from the viewer's responding spirit
some other aspect which is of genuine consequence."

Matisse had got to know German Expressionist work in Munich
and especially in Berlin when he toured Germany with Purrmann in
1908. Now he painted works such as 'The Algerian Woman' (p. 35),
weighted by the use of contrastive shapes, crisp contours, and a
luminous ground, and harder in their expressiveness. Ernst Ludwig
Kirchner and Erich Heckel took a similar approach, making their
colours vivid to the point of dissonance and subjecting ornamentally
flat areas of colour to the powerful discipline of angular lines.

But contrasts were only one of the means Matisse used to achieve
his effects. Another was the simplification of objects so that they
could be rendered in a few straight and curved lines. This principle is
at work in 'Flowers and Ceramic Plate' (right), where one contrast
between curved and rectangular is heightened by a second between
the dominant blue and the plate's green. The pot and the plate are
each given a distinct character, and the curled-up sheet of paper
marks a compromise between polarities. The black shadows link
opposites, and serve to define them against the prevailing blue.

Matisse spent the winter of 1910/1911 in Spain, mainly in Seville
and in his hotel room in that city he painted his 'Spanish Still Life
(Seville II)'. The close-up view of sofa and round table has the effect of
a still life. We are so close to the subject that little can be seen of the
wallpaper and floor: the table and sofa are draped in materials, and it
is the heavy ornamentation on these that dominates the painting. The
pomegranates and peppers that are scattered about do nothing to
diminish this impact. If anything here has any autonomy it is the large
white flowerpot; the flowers themselves, on the other hand, are barely
distinguishable from the patterns behind. The figure and the
background are of equal status.

When he returned from Seville to Issy-les-Moulineaux, Matisse
had his wife act as his model. For quite a time, his family provided

Flowers and Ceramic Plate, 1911
Oil on canvas, 93.5 x 82.5 cm
Städelsches Kunstinstitut und
Städtische Galerie, Frankfurt am Main

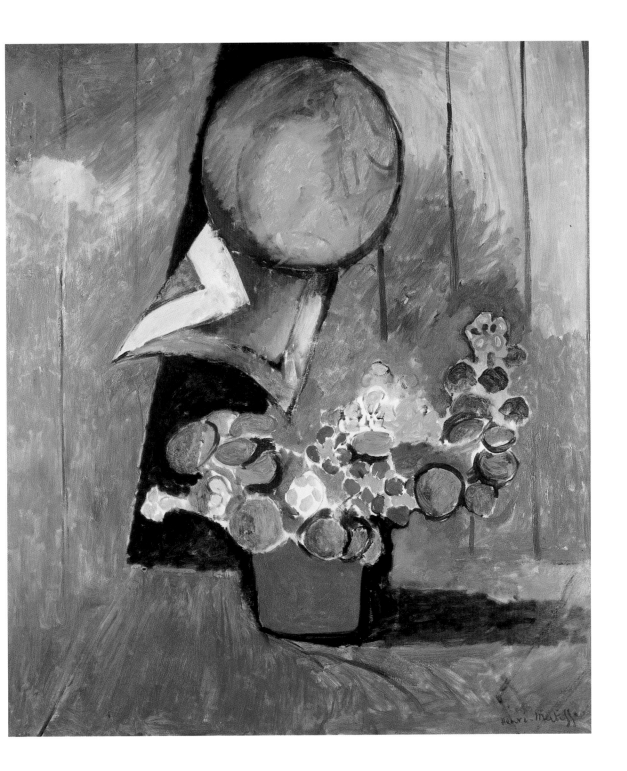

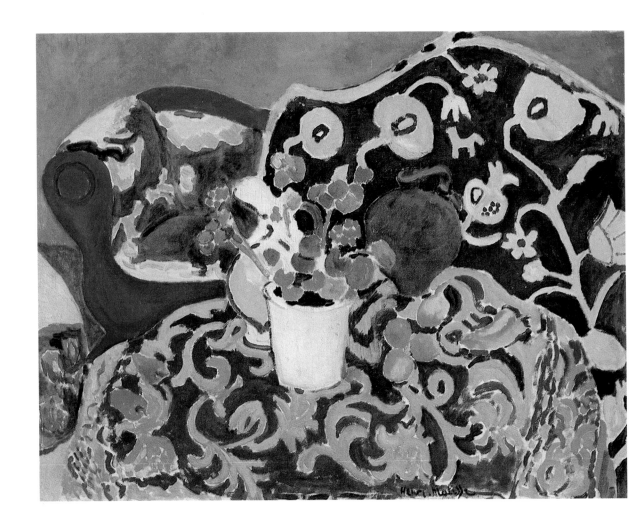

Spanish Still Life (Seville II), 1911
Oil on canvas, 89 x 116 cm
Hermitage, Leningrad

"As far as the still life is concerned: the painter's
task is to reproduce the colour qualities of the
objects in his composition, by staying alert and
sensitive to the shifting values of colour tones and
their inter-relations ... Merely copying the object
is not art. What counts is to express the emotion
they call forth in you, the feeling they awaken, the
relations established between the objects ..."
HENRI MATISSE

Matisse with a constant and free source of models who responded
with understanding to his wishes. His wife Amélie patiently wore the
costumes and struck the poses the artist required. Her involvement
and interest, qualities all too rarely shared by professional models,
gave her a serious dignity which is visible in the paintings even when
an exotic costume reduces her to a mere "extra". The 'Manila Shawl'
is the main motif of that painting (p. 41), rather than the woman
wearing it. The floral pattern of the shawl contrasts with the blue
background and the red floor, which meet at a diagonal. There is a
greater physical presence in this human figure than in the objects in
the 'Spanish Still Life': something of a compromise has been reached
between the principle of decorative abstraction and that of
three-dimensional realism.

The painter's family life was sternly subordinated to his artistic needs. At table, Madame Matisse would ask the children to be quiet, so as not to disturb their father's concentration on an important painting. Doubtless the family had no easy time of it under Matisse's disciplined regimen – but neither did Matisse himself. His own obsessiveness, the experiments with new approaches to configuration, and the dangers of failure, all tormented Matisse. While he was at work on 'The Painter's Family' (p. 39) he wrote to Michael Stein: "Everything is going well, though until I am finished I cannot say anything. It may sound illogical, but I am not certain of my success. This all-or-nothing wears me away."

'The Painter's Family', painted at Issy-les-Moulineaux, shows the Matisse family in silent harmony, all about their own business: the two sons Jean and Pierre are playing draughts, daughter Marguerite is pausing to reflect on the book she is reading, and the artist's wife is

PAGE 40:
Moroccan Landscape (Acanthus), 1912
Oil on canvas, 115 x 80 cm
Moderna Museet, Stockholm

PAGE 41:
Manila Shawl, 1911
Oil on canvas, 118 x 75 cm
Kunstmuseum, Basle

The Painter's Family, 1911
Oil on canvas, 143 x 194 cm
Hermitage, Leningrad

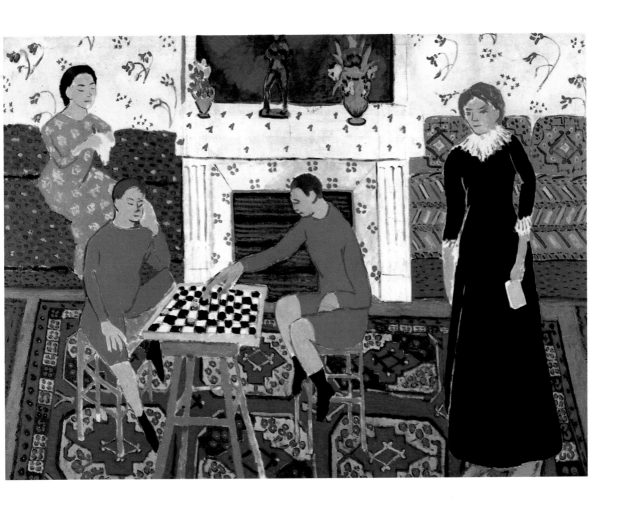

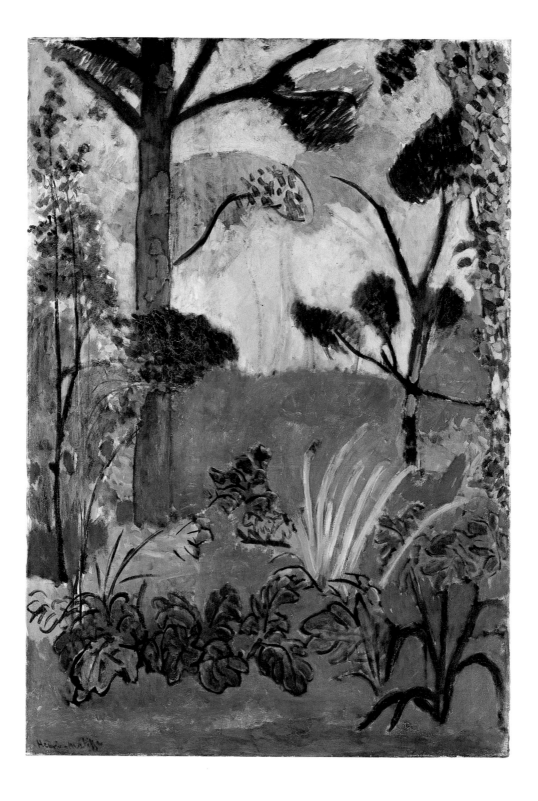

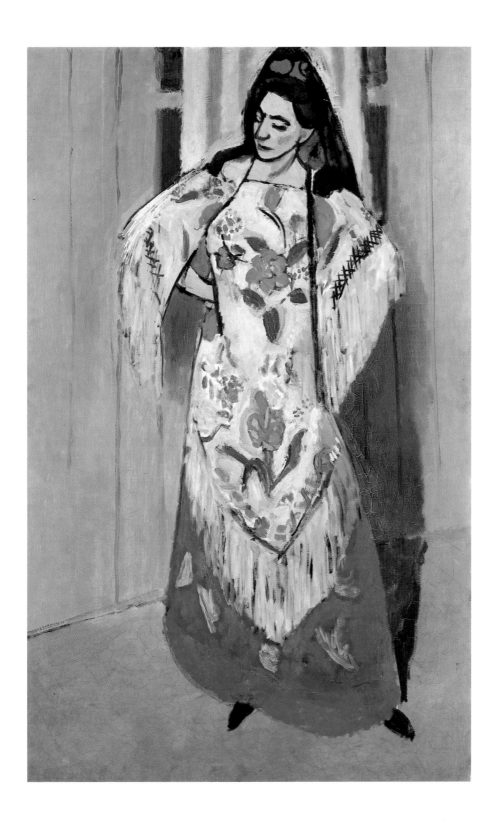

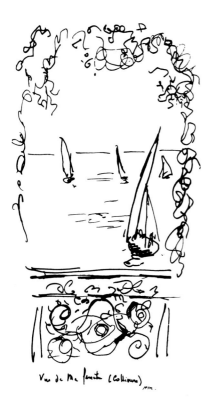

Landscape at Tangier, viewed through a Window, 1912
Pen and ink

Still Life with Oranges, 1913
Oil on canvas, 94 x 83 cm
Musée National du Louvre, Paris
(gifted by Picasso)

concentrating on her embroidery, seated on a divan. Madame Matisse and her daughter are distinguished as individuals; the two brothers, on the other hand, have lost their identity, and their identical red clothing makes them seem two halves of a single image. The visual echo transforms a realistic image into abstract signs. All four people are surrounded by a surfeit of ornament. Most important is the carpet, the oriental presence, the variegated pattern of which infects the entire room: sofas, cushions, walls, and indeed the fireplace. The lavishly decorated surfaces contrast rhythmically in line and colour. The only quietening element is introduced by repetition: even the removal of the boys' individual characters by means of repetition enhances this quiet. Jean and Pierre frame the draughts board at the painting's centre and emblematically sum up the design of the whole picture. Matisse has fitted his family into a decorative design.

Matisse spent the winters of 1911 and 1912 in Morocco, and claimed that these periods abroad renewed his contact with Nature and that his new impressions rejuvenated and energized him: "My Moroccan travels helped me make the necessary transition. They also gave me a closer contact with Nature than was possible if I continue to apply the vigorous yet limited theory that Fauvism had become." The luxuriant southern greenery of gardens in Tangier gave him wha his art needed. Suddenly a new light blazed in his paintings. Writing from Tangier, Matisse told his fellow-painter Camoin: "It is such mild light, quite different from Mediterranean light." Later he was to recall that on his arrival it had rained incessantly for a whole month, till at last the grey parted and revealed a green clean as a freshly-opened almond.

For six weeks, Matisse worked in the vast park of the Villa Bronx. He painted three pictures in identical format, pictures which can be seen as a triptych: 'Moroccan Landscape (Acanthus)' (p. 40), 'Moroccan Garden (Periwinkles)' (Private Collection), and 'The Palm Leaf, Tangier' (National Gallery of Art, Washington D.C.). In the western tradition in art, triptychs have religious connotations: they are the most common form of Christian altar painting and have an aura of glory. Marcel Sembat, a politician and Parisian deputy who had been collecting Matisse since 1908 and advocated his art in magazines, wrote the first monograph on the artist in 1920, in which he noted that these three garden scenes represent a kind of transfiguration that comes close to a religious spirit.

The second Moroccan sojourn (1912/13), when Matisse was joined by Camoin, also produced the 'Still Life with Oranges' (p. 43). A basket of oranges is on a table draped in a cloth with a floral pattern. In the background hangs a mauve curtain, its folds stiff. In 1944, Picasso was to buy this painting, with its violent colour clashes, out of a private collection. Oranges are often to be found in Matisse's work, and prompted Guillaume Apollinaire to remark: "If Matisse's work can

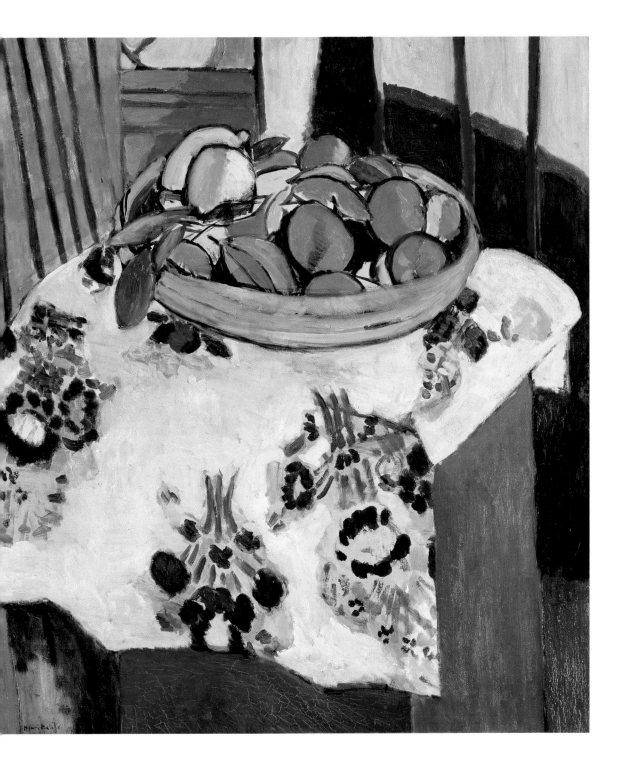

be compared to anything, then to an orange. Like the orange, Henri Matisse's paintings are the fruit of dazzling light."

Matisse did not return to Tangier. He wanted to work in Paris. He was not happy with the decision, though: the "gloomy sky" was so oppressive, and a short period spent in the South of France accompanying his mother (who had heart trouble) to Menton re-awakened his longing for the south. But then he found a place to live on his old Quai Saint-Michel, and his Paris concentration triumphed over the temptations of the exotic. Matisse was also afraid of succumbing to routine: in the light of familiarity, grass would not seem as fresh, people not as alive, the very light not so bright. He wanted to let his experience mature.

On 3rd August, 1914, the First World War broke out. Matisse was in Paris, and was terrified. The family home was destroyed in the German attack, and Matisse could get no news of his mother, who was confined to Bohain, or of his brother, who had been taken away by the Germans along with all the other menfolk of the village. He wrote to Purrmann: "This war has conferred a seriousness on the lives even of those who are taking no part in it, if they can imagine the feelings of a simple soldier who loses his life without quite knowing why, though he feels the sacrifice is right."

The effect the war had on Matisse's art can only be grasped if we consider the stringent colour scale that is characteristic of his work during the war years, and the increased tendency to simplification (which, it is true, had long been present). In 1914 the streamlining of forms into geometrical basics such as squares, rectangles, circles and ovals peaked, and continued through 1916. It cannot be coincidental that the painting which shows his geometrical simplification at its most extreme is the 'View of Notre-Dame' (right). This painting is the culmination of a long series of views Matisse did from the fifth floor of the house in the Quai Saint-Michel. They were done from the window, and the right-hand jamb appears as a vertical in the picture. Together with the diagonal lines, which imply depth, the verticals and horizontals add up to an abstract structure on a blue ground, the effect of which is intensified by the green bush. It is as if Matisse were seeking refuge from the real world in the geometry of the church.

Not long before the Battle of the Marne, Matisse resolved to leave Paris and travel with Marquet to join his daughter Marguerite in Toulouse and from there continue to Collioure. Marquet and the Matisse family lived at Collioure until November 1914. Juan Gris, who had found lodgings with the tutor of Matisse's children, remained even longer.

It was a time of fear, and the Cubists and Fauvists laid their less weighty, aesthetic conflicts aside. Cubism confirmed Matisse in his move toward geometrical simplicity: basic and permanent forms seemed a way of responding to the tragedy of the age. So too was the

View of Notre-Dame, 1914
Oil on canvas, 147.3 x 94.3 cm
Museum of Modern Art, New York

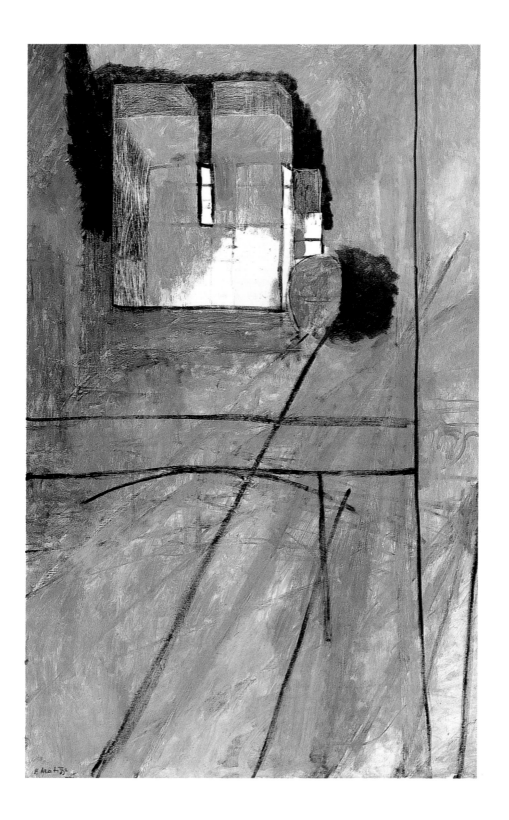

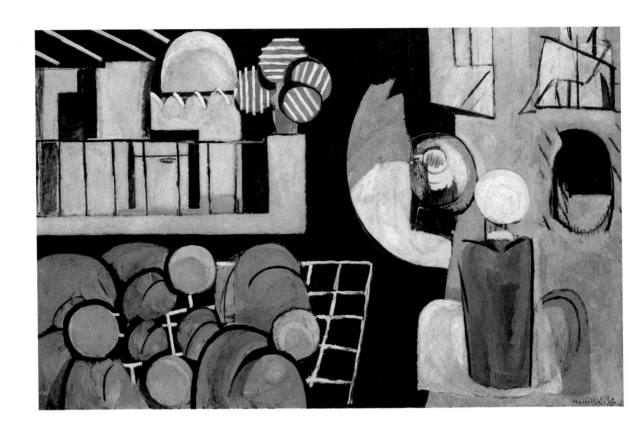

The Moroccans, 1916
Oil on canvas, 181.3 x 279.4 cm
Museum of Modern Art, New York

RIGHT:
French Window at Collioure, 1914
Oil on canvas, 116.5 x 88 cm
Musée National d'Art Moderne,
Centre Georges Pompidou, Paris

darkening in Matisse's colours: the sunny shades disappeared, and during the war black occupied the place that had been given to almond-green during the Morocco period. In 'French Window at Collioure' (right) black covers everything apart from the rectangular frame, as if the views Matisse loved to see from windows had been hit by black-out regulations. All that remains on the left is a grey-blue vertical strip with a black border, and on the right one grey-brown and one blue-green vertical strip, separated by a black line. Nothing else is left of the window and shutters. The spatial sense is kept to a minimum. The diagonal line across the grey-brown base gives a rudimentary perspective: we recognise the trapezoid shape at the bottom as the floor. This is the closest Matisse ever gets to a total abstraction in which geometrical forms and pictorial zones coincide.

Matisse returned from Collioure in November 1914 and settled, working at the Quai Saint-Michel in Paris and at Issy-les-Moulineaux Black continued to be dominant in 'The Moroccans' (p. 46), the last of his Moroccan series. Matisse reflected on his happiness in that country: "It became clear to me that my sole sanctuary was the fairly lasting memories I have of Morocco." The bright, colourful memories

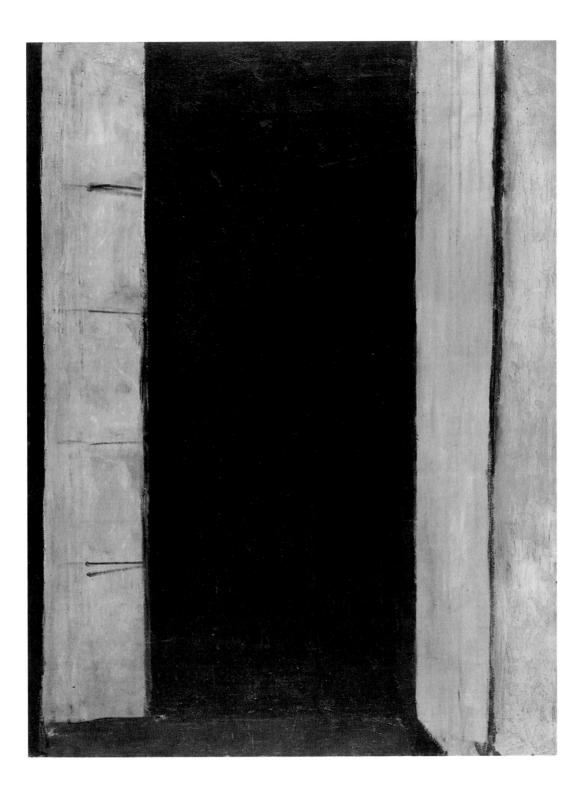

The Window (Interior with Forget-me-nots), 1916
Oil on canvas, 146 x 116.8 cm
Detroit Institute of Arts, Detroit

of happiness are seen against the background of black times. The vision of paradise in 'The Moroccans' is in three isolated motifs: the pumpkins in the garden, the balcony with flowers, and the gathering of men. It is a painting governed by the tart counterpointing of straight and curved lines. The unity of the earlier Moroccan pictures is gone.

At the same time Matisse began painting interiors and still lifes again. The work he painted in Paris during the winter consisted mainly of darker, richer colours with black shadows; what he painted during the more congenial seasons, at Issy-les-Moulineaux, came out brighter. 'The Window (Interior with Forget-me-nots)' (right) is a typical example. The objects shown are still parts of a geometrical design.

In summer 1917 Jean and Pierre Matisse went to war: Pierre to an armour division, Jean to the air force ground staff. The Matisse family began to loosen; the children were adults now, going their own ways. Once the war was over, life was no longer lived together, and Matisse responded by withdrawing even more wholly into his work. At one point, when two of his children were visiting, he wrote to his friend Camoin: "My children Marguerite and Pierre are here, which is pleasant, but nonetheless I do work better when I'm on my own."

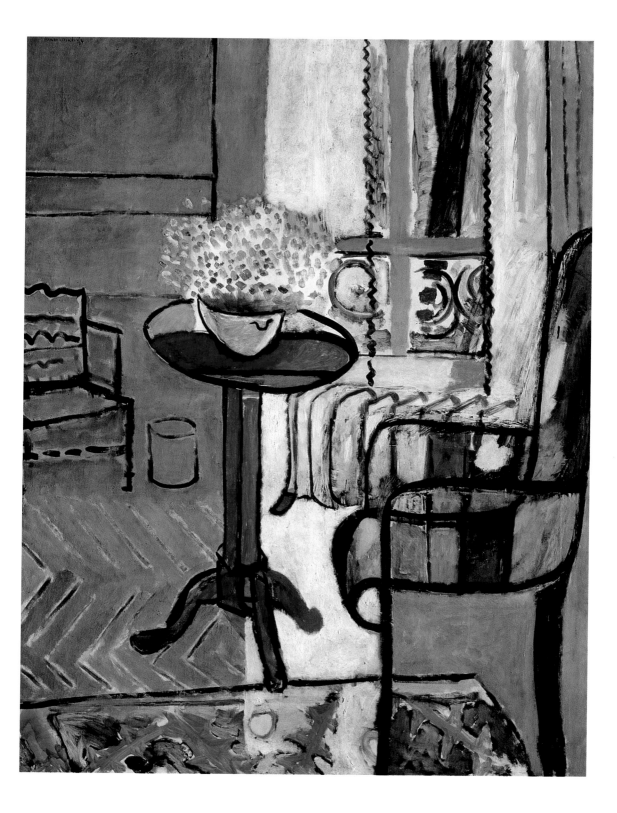

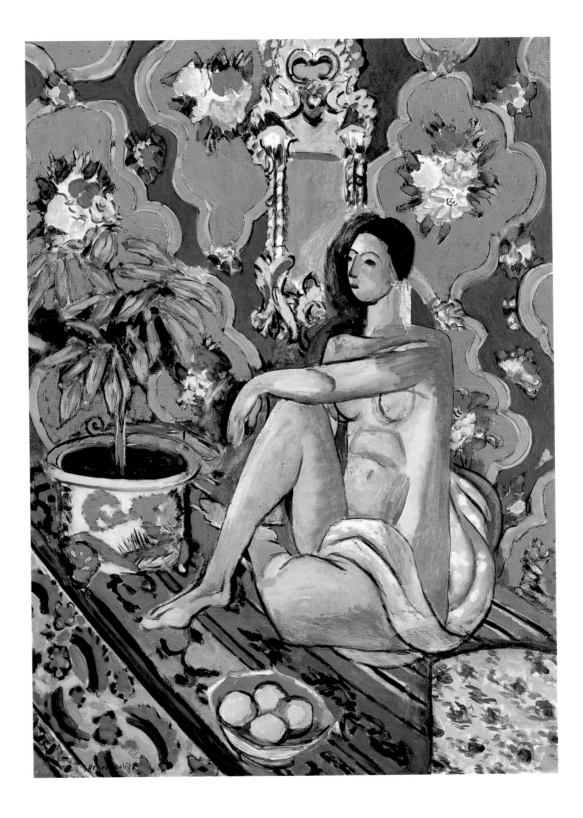

The Intimacy of the Nice Period
1917-1929

In 1916, while the First World War was still taking its bloody course, Matisse had first visited the Côte d'Azur, almost by chance, his doctor having advised a stay in Menton to help his bronchitis. Matisse broke his journey in Nice; and, though he made the move only for the winter months, he gradually shifted part of his creative life from the north to the south, in a spirit of flight from reality. Later, Matisse commented: "Nice is all décor, a very beautiful, fragile town but a town without people, without depth." As Pierre Schneider, author of the most authoritative work on Matisse, concludes: "one cannot help noticing a lowering of tension during the first decade in Nice, a certain loss of direction which was periodically expressed in a kind of melancholy. The cause lay in the artist's evading the very things that would have justified his recourse to realism: the weight of reality, its resistance, its refusal to comply with the purely formal demands of painting. The family was the guardian of the meaningfulness of reality; its removal led to a flattening of reality, a lack of significance in realism."

In fact, a climate of aesthetic slackness was becoming generally noticeable in France. Picasso turned to classicism; Derain returned to a mood of order; Fernand Léger entered on his "monumental" phase. In Italy, the school of "pittura metafisica", and the Futurist Gino Severini, returned to tradition. On the other hand, during the war the artists of Russian Suprematism and the Dutch "De Stijl" movement joined forces in the hope of creating a new world and ending the separation of the two cultures, artistic and technological. 1919 saw the beginning of the Bauhaus in Germany. All areas of modern life were to be newly formed: the fine arts, architecture and urban planning, printing and advertising, photography and cinema. The new arts were ruled by geometric forms. And the artists were new artists, of a younger generation, while Matisse found himself at an advanced stage in his own development.

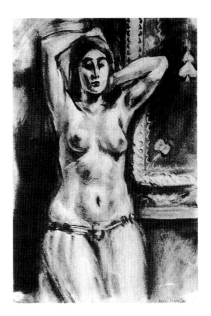

Standing Female Nude, 1923/24
Charcoal, 47.6 x 31.5 cm
Musée National d'Art Moderne,
Centre Georges Pompidou, Paris

LEFT:
**Decorative Figure on an
Ornamental Background, 1925**
Oil on canvas, 131 x 98 cm
Musée National d'Art Moderne
Centre Georges Pompidou, Paris

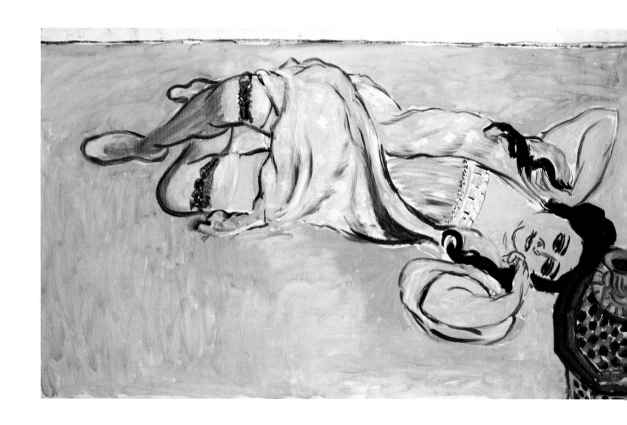

Laurette with a Coffee Cup, 1917
Oil on canvas, 89 x 146 cm
Private collection

RIGHT:
Laurette's Head, with a Coffee Cup, 1917
Oil on canvas, 92 x 73 cm
Kunstmuseum, Solothurn

Now, after all his daring experiments, Matisse was aiming to create harmony out of what he had discovered. He himself expresse his position like this: "I had spent long and tiring years in experimenting, and had done everything in my power to fashion the conflicts into a new harmony in a work, with a new and unparallele power. I had also worked very hard on commissioned murals and major projects. And meanwhile my painting, that had started in luxuriance, had established a new clarity and simplicity of its own. What was obvious was a tendency to abstraction of colour, and a lo of rich, warm, generous form: arabesques were emerging dominant Out of this duality was born an art that went beyond my own inner limits and achieved a reconciliation of opposites. And I was in need c a breathing-space, quiet, a recuperative spell far from Paris and my cares. The odalisques were born of this contented longing: a beautifu living dream, and an experience known in ecstasy, by day and nigh in the magic of a climate."

Matisse's need to relax is expressed in the tremendous wearines of his odalisques. They also represented a return to a greater realism For Matisse at this date, and still more for Picasso, Jean Auguste

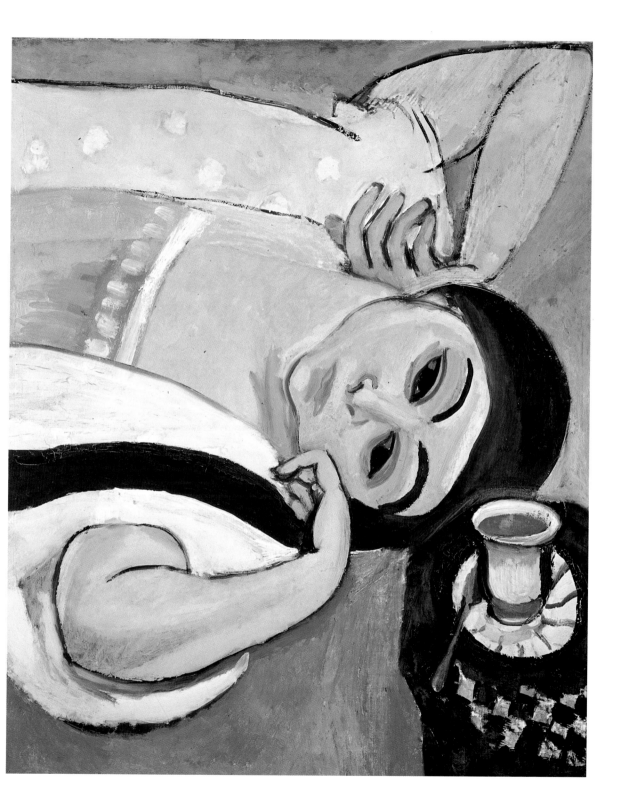

Dominique Ingres and Gustave Courbet were the historical examples to be followed: the former because of his precise draughtmanship and tendency to render a painting into planes, the latter because of his amassing of colour.

For several years an Italian woman called Laurette was Matisse's favourite model, and he portrayed her in a number of works: full-length studies, portraits, nudes. In 'Laurette with a Coffee Cup' (p. 52) she is soft, her lines flowing. The horizontality of her relaxed position is complemented by the vertical of the table with the coffee cup, which also defines the painting's spatial qualities. The black of her hair, of the table and contouring, keeps the woman from merging wholly into shades of brighter grey and muted green. 'Laurette's Head, with a Coffee Cup' (p. 53) intensifies the contrasts. The close-up has the effect of a detail; the shapes are tighter and simpler, the colours and lines both stronger. Here once again it is the coffee cup that defines spatial relations. Laurette's proportions have been altered to emphasize the weight in her reclining position. We see her close-up, yet her body remains within flat dimensions. Her wide-open eyes are looking neither at painter nor at viewer: she seems to be dreaming.

In 1916/17, when Matisse was living at the Hotel Beaurivage in Nice, he was anxious lest the chambermaid shift his easel, and so took to laying out a red string or other marker on the carpet so that he could locate the exact position again. Matisse needed a clearly defined, unchanging reality. He needed it in order to close the gap between the brief impression and the lasting expression.

Every year from the end of May until September he would return to Paris, and work in his studio at Issy-les-Moulineaux. 'Garden at Issy' (right), with its green leafage and the round pond with Matisse' well-loved goldfish swimming in it, is an almost totally abstract composition in warm browns and greens. Matisse has painted his subject at an angle that suggests we are looking from a window high up. This tilting of the angle is recurrent in Matisse and preserves a sense of planes. The individual elements are placed on the brown ground like items in a cut-out, though with some shadow-modelling to give them distinct body. It is as if parts of a stage set were in the picture. The tension between realistic and abstract is unresolved but wholly productive.

When dealing with landscape, or with any external reality, Matisse preferred to interpose a distancing effect between himself and his subject – a room, balcony or railing. The Impressionists liked to paint from Nature. Matisse, who rated expression above impression and decoration above realism, painted his major works in his studio. In Nice, his studio was his hotel room: for example, when he painted 'Interior with a Violin Case' (p. 57) he was living in the Hotel de la Méditerranée, which he valued especially on account of its theatrical

Garden at Issy, 1917 – 1919
Oil on canvas, 130 x 89 cm
Private collection

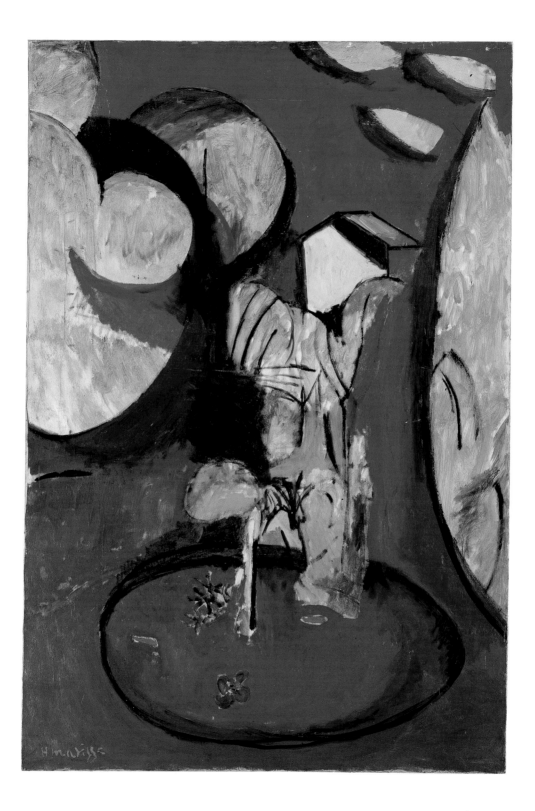

décor and furnishing: "Of course it was a grand old hotel! Such wonderful Italian stucco on the ceilings! What tiled floors! Demolishing that building was a great mistake. I stayed there for four years, for the sheer pleasure of painting there. Do you remember the light coming in through the blinds? It was all artificial, absurd, delightful, magnificent." The bright light from outside enters at the open balcony door; the inside of the violin case reflects the blue of sky and sea; the slant perspective draws our gaze to what lies outside. In the treatment of the rear wall, even in the colour values and the brightness of the painting, we sense Matisse's openness to natural spatial terms and a resistance to the closed-off unity of purely decorative art.

The resistance offered by reality to abstraction is a theme in many of Matisse's paintings. In 'The Lorrain Chair' (p. 58), for example, the chair and bowl of peaches are seen at a three-dimensional angle which creates a tension with the flat, frontal background. The Jouy linen is no longer vividly coloured nor strict in line. The red-brown Lorrain chair, on the other hand, is more exactly delineated but too insubstantial to assert a full presence; nor is the still life solid enough to prevail over the background. The light, transparent colouring mediates between the polarities.

Matisse's work continued to be his life, as we can see from the intrusion of the studio into the interior of 'The Painting Lesson' (p. 59). Living and working had become one. "A painter exists solely by virtue of his paintings," he wrote. The painter's presence within his work disturbs this notion, in that it introduces a realistic, biographical element. For this reason, his presence in 'The Painting Lesson' is kept to a minimum – the painter appears only as a drawing, with neither weight, solidity nor colour. This optical effect links the painter to his milieu but at the same time emphasizes his distance from it. And in reflecting on his own activity, the painter reinforces his own position as sovereign creator of his imaged world. The presentation of the painter is partly removed into an unreal, conceptual realm, but the presence of the reading girl is strengthened. Poring over her open book, she connects with the still life of vase, fruits and brush on the table. The black of the printed book and of the brush creates a further connection, with the background, while the oval mirror reaches out to include a landscape that is otherwise excluded from the room. This projected image, in the mirror, is in fact a picture-within-a-picture, and serves as an allusion to the painter's work. It mediates between him and his model. The painting's various levels – areas of drawing and of painting, and the reflection in the mirror – are united by means of the colour and light effects, to create a two-dimensional harmony.

Matisse was looking for a new synthesis. As he put it in 1919: "I worked as an Impressionist, directly from Nature. Then I tried for concentration, an intense expression in line and colour. In the

Interior with a Violin Case, 1918/19
Oil on canvas, 97.3 x 60 cm
Museum of Modern Art, New York

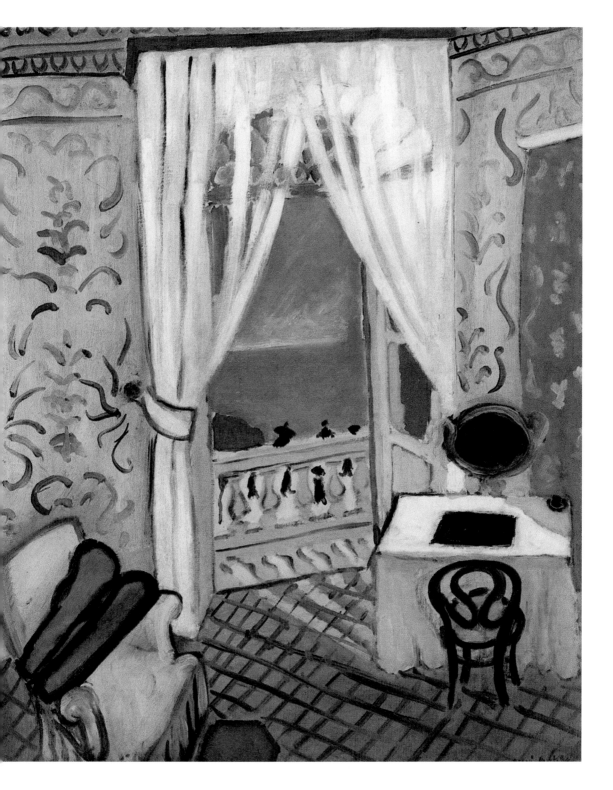

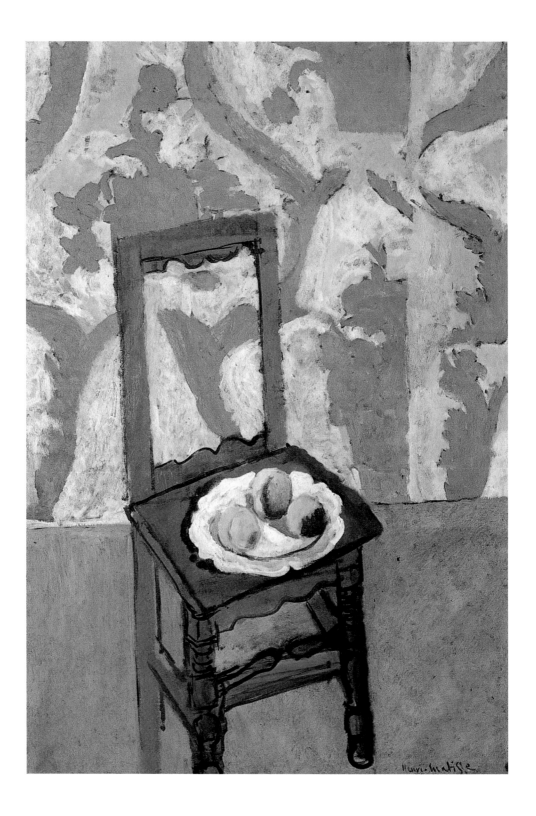

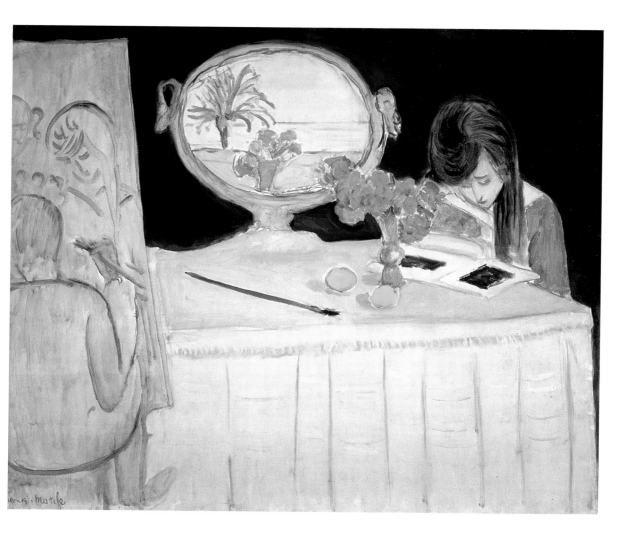

The Painting Lesson, 1919
Oil on canvas, 74 x 93 cm
Scottish National Gallery
of Modern Art, Edinburgh

LEFT:
The Lorrain Chair, 1919
Oil on canvas, 130 x 89 cm
Private collection

process, other values are naturally lost: the solidity of matter, spatial depth, the wealth of detail. What I want to do now is bring it all together." It was this synthesis that he was after when he painted 'The Black Table' (right) at Issy-les-Moulineaux in summer 1919. His model Antoinette appears amid voluptuous, grand patterning: on the walls one restrained wallpaper is beside another more lively one, while the floor consists of broad diagonals. Patterns tend to confine the objects they adorn to a flat plane. On the table there is a big bouquet of flowers. The most powerful contrast is between the black of the table and the white of the woman's clothing, and this contrast is echoed in the foliate patterning on the wall. For all the painting's abundant detail, it retains a certain contained clarity thanks to this black and white.

In the 1920s this use of a greater sense of reality, spatial depth, and wealth of detail grew in Matisse, in paintings such as 'Odalisque in Red Trousers' (pp. 62/63). By now, Matisse was established and officially recognized, and the painting was bought by the Musée du Luxembourg in Paris soon after its completion. Matisse himself was awarded the cross of the legion of honour. Perhaps such recognition was connected with the seeming conventionality of the odalisques. Certainly Matisse felt he needed to defend them against such a charge: "Take a close look at these odalisques. Sunlight rules, triumphant and splendid, and soaks up the colours and shapes. The oriental decoration of the interiors, the splendour of the wall and floor carpets, the voluptuous costumes, the sensuality of these heavy, drowsy bodies, the lazy expectancy in their eyes, all the magnificence of the siesta with arabesques and colours pushed to their limits – none of this should fool you: I have never cared for the merely anecdotal. Beneath this mood of languishing relaxation and sun-filled sensuality which includes the people and objects alike there is a great tension which is purely an artistic, painterly tension and exists in the interplay between the elements in the painting." The 'Odalisque in Red Trousers' is the best example of what Matisse meant by painterly interplay: powerful shades of colour are opposed to tender, muted shades, the flat anti-spatial rear wall with its ornate adornment is matched by the full three-dimensionality of the odalisque reclining on the couch. The young woman's delicate body, with the arms in different positions and one leg tucked under the other, has a physical plasticity.

The odalisque in red trousers has a solid presence against the decorative environment which the 'Decorative Figure on an Ornamental Background' (p. 50) is unable to achieve in her jungle of colour and detail. The French baroque wallpaper is of an extremely bombastic character, and the overall tastelessness of the multiplicity of styles in this room becomes an oppressive tableau of shrilly insistent motifs. The room is so decorative it becomes menacing. The

The Black Table, 1919
Oil on canvas, 100 x 81 cm
Private collection, Switzerland

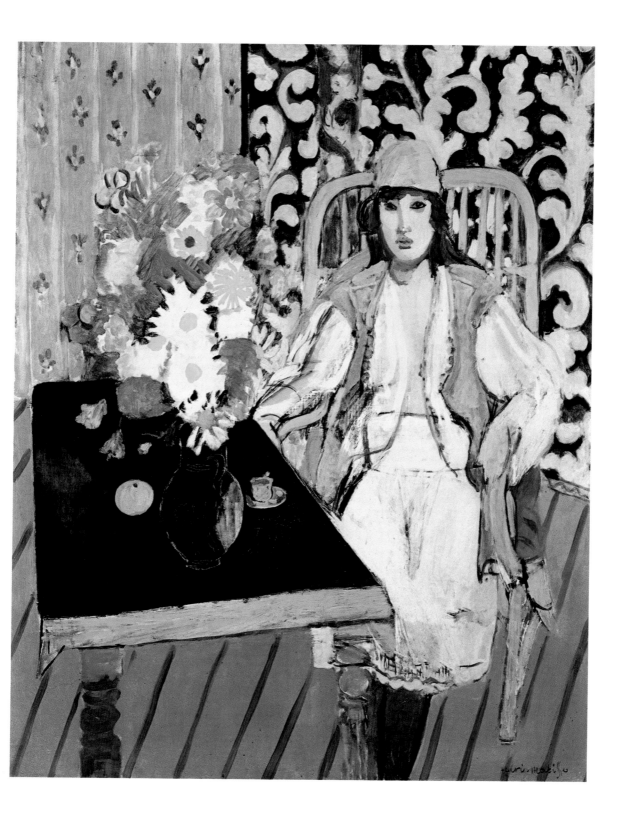

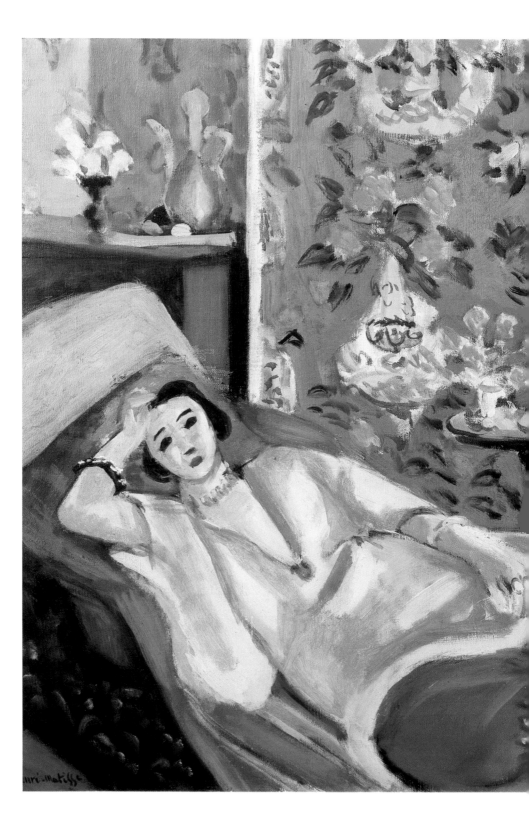

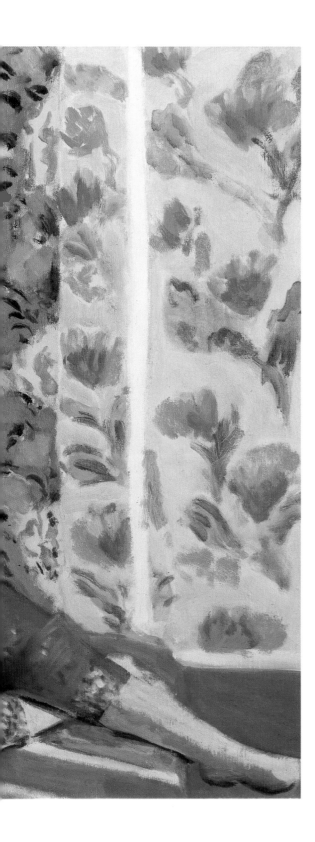

"The portrait is one of the most curious art forms. It demands special qualities in the artist, and an almost total kinship with the model. The painter must have no preconceived notion of the model – his spirit must be open and receive everything, just as in a landscape he would take in every one of the scents on the air." HENRI MATISSE

Odalisque in Red Trousers, 1924/25
Oil on canvas, 50 x 61 cm
Musée de l'Orangerie des Tuileries, Paris

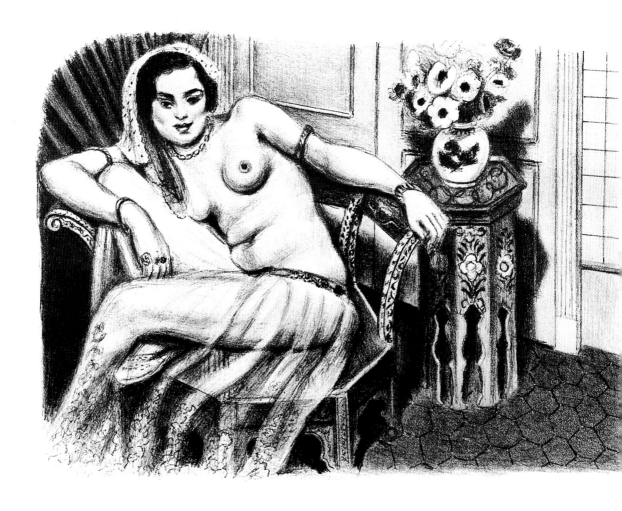

Odalisque in a Gauze Skirt, 1929
Black and white lithograph, 29 x 38 cm
Private collection, Paris

potted plant and the dish of fruit are flat and vanish into the décor. The seated woman, described by Matisse as a "decorative figure", is trying not to be suffocated. The parts of her body are like cylinders, like parts of some living machine. The base of the body is broadened by the leg angled under: this shifts the centre of gravity and has the effect of anchoring the figure firmly in position on the floor. The body's position highlights the rear verticals and the horizontals of the floor, and its straight and angled lines echo the straight and angled lines in the walls and floor, which might otherwise not be as apparent. The position of the figure's legs corresponds to the angling of the floor. At the top, a shadow gives depth and volume to the figure where it is seen against the background. The contrast between a right-angled figure and an arabesque background gives Matisse the opportunity to preserve depth in a decorative space. Never before – nor ever after – did Matisse so signally oppose sculptural and decorative elements or so sharply challenge his viewer's perceptive responses.

64

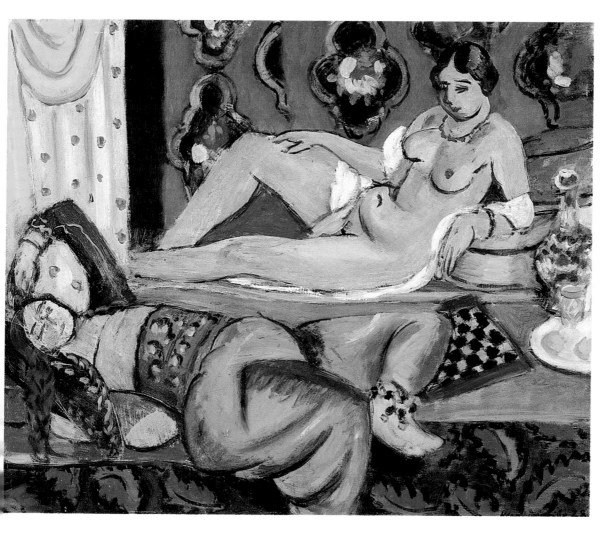

In 'Odalisques' the tension between realism and decoration
is diminished. Their physical substantiality is slight, and
they merge flatly into the environment; the baroque wallpaper is
triumphant. In showing one naked and one clothed odalisque,
Matisse in fact reduces their individuality through the repetition, as if
they were the positive and negative of a single pattern. The superficial
splendour of a hotel-room Eden is on its way out.

Odalisques, 1928
Oil on canvas, 54 x 65 cm
Moderna Museet, Stockholm

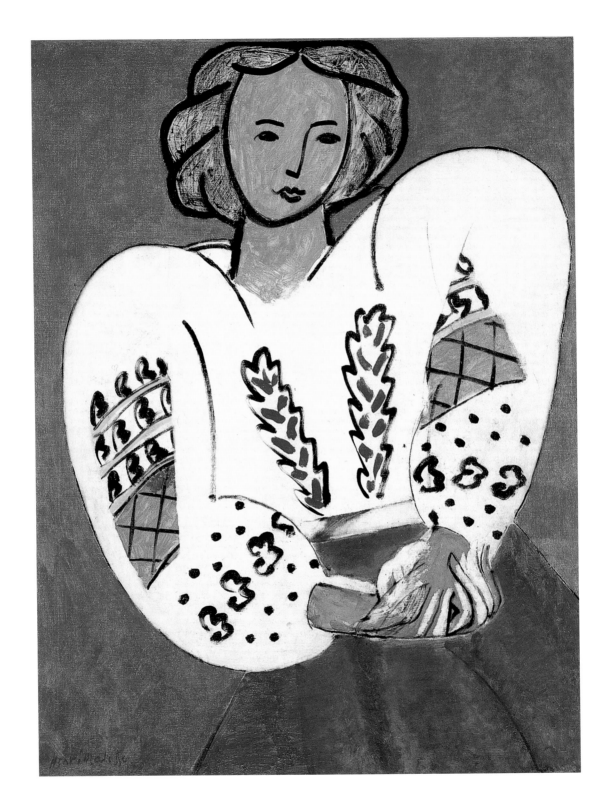

Beyond Spatial Limits
1930-1940

Matisse referred to his numerous journeys as merely "changing places": the only time he felt he was genuinely going on his "travels" was in February 1930 when he journeyed to Tahiti via New York and San Francisco. He was enthusiastic about New York: "If I weren't accustomed to sticking to a decision once it's made I should stay in New York. It really is a new world, vast and majestic as the ocean. There is a sense of great human energy being released."

America fascinated him. But he went on, and took ship to Tahiti. His stay there was not of immediate profit in his work; under the influence of the constant quality of the light he succumbed to indolence and boredom, and in a mood well-nigh melancholy wrote: "It is all pretty banal. I feel quite remote from it, and the only consolation I can find is to tell myself that I am experiencing a real tranquility of the spirit, such as I have never known before. Certainly I can see the extraordinary things here, but I tire of them quickly. In my mind I am still more in France than here – I see the house, and the work I have left behind, with a greater and more feeling intensity than my present surroundings ... Nor do I care about the people at all. I don't say this will not prove to have been of use for me when I am home again, but now I find it hard to believe. I do not know why, but here you never feel the urge to move or think – that, I suppose, is why I see it as tranquillity."

On his return journey in September 1930 Matisse visited his most important collector in the USA, Albert Barnes, at Merion. Barnes had a private museum, the Barnes Foundation, where masterpieces by Seurat, Cézanne, Renoir and Matisse hung, and he now asked Matisse to decorate the lunettes above the three French windows in the main hall. The painter accepted the challenge, and laid down this guiding principle: "It would have been inappropriate to treat my decorative work like any other painting. I was aiming to adapt my fresco to cement and stone. I do not think this is very often attempted

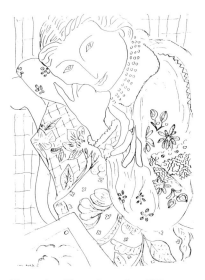

Woman in a Blouse, Dreaming, 1936
Pen and ink

LEFT:
The Rumanian Blouse, 1940
Oil on canvas, 92 x 73 cm
Musée National d'Art Moderne,
Centre Georges Pompidou, Paris

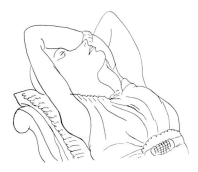

Woman Sleeping, 1936
Pen and ink

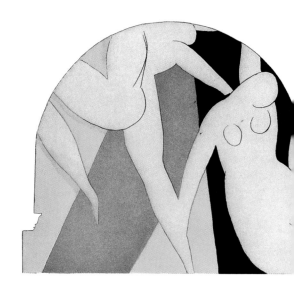

nowadays. People who paint on walls now create paintings and not true murals."

Before he began his labours, Matisse returned once more to Merion, at the end of 1930, to make sure of the exact measurements of the area. For his subject he again chose a motif from 'La Joie de Vivre' (which hung at Merion), the dance (above). Matisse had 52 square metres to cover, and to produce work on this scale he rented an old film studio in Nice.

Preparation took a long time: he had problems with the distribution of colours. For the first time he used coloured paper, cut to the required shape. Matisse wrote: "For three years my work consisted in shifting eleven areas of colour around, like moving pieces in a game of draughts. The colours were paper cut-outs; and it took me that long to establish an arrangement that I found satisfactory." The figures too were cut out, in a pale grey paper (against the coloured background), and again it took Matisse time before he achieved the desired simplicity. By 1932 he had finally found the balance he wished between the drawn figures and the colours, and he began to transfer the composition to canvas – and only then did he discover that a mistake had been made in measuring the Merion lunettes. Rather than correct his work, Matisse started anew. He was suffering from acute nephritis and sheer exhaustion, but pressed on with work on the first version, which he had completed by the end of 1933.

The figures from 'La Joie de Vivre' and the Shchukin 'La Danse' appear here in a freer constellation, as a series of arabesque shapes against the geometrical colour zones of the background. The limited

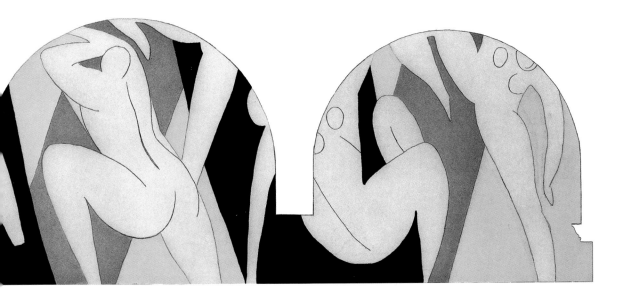

range of colours – blue, pink, grey and black – intensifies the effect of clarity and flatness. The figures refuse to remain confined in the limited areas of the lunettes, and require the viewer's imagination to go beyond the given spatial limits. Matisse observed: "What was most important was to call forth a sense of measureless infinity in a confined space."

For Matisse, seeing the work installed at Merion brought a sense of relief. The necessary unity of wall-space and image had been achieved. As proud as any father, Matisse wrote jubilantly: "The decoration is in position. It is truly glorious – you can have no conception of it until you have seen it. The whole arched ceiling radiates, and the effect even extends down to the floor. I am extremely tired but very pleased. Having seen the picture in place, I now feel disconnected from it. It has become part of the building; and I no longer think of the work that has gone into it, the past. It has acquired its own independent existence. This was a real birth, and the mother delivered herself of all the pain of the past."

After his wearying labours at 'The Dance', Matisse took a cure in Abano in Italy, and visited Padua to see Giotto's frescoes again. The return to a decorative style heralded by 'The Dance' continued. In the years that followed, Matisse worked on tapestry projects and book illustrations. A series of etchings of scenes from the 'Odyssey' were done to illustrate James Joyce's 'Ulysses', and he drew a great deal.

Matisse had always drawn a lot. But after 1930 it became a particularly important medium in his quest for simplicity. As early as 1908 he had published his programmatic essay 'A Painter's Notes',

The Dance (first version), 1931 – 1933
Oil on canvas: three portions,
340 x 387 cm, 355 x 498 cm, 333 x 391 cm
Musée d'Art Moderne de la Ville de Paris, Paris

"Perhaps it is important to add that the composition is the result of the actual confrontation of the painter and fifty-two square metres of space. The first step was for my spirit to take hold of this space. I didn't use the modern method of blowing up a composition by projecting it to scale and transferring it on tracing paper.
A man trying to track an aeroplane across the sky with a searchlight does not trace the same passage through the sky as the pilot does. I hope I am expressing this correctly and that you will see how vast a difference there is between the two approaches."   HENRI MATISSE

69

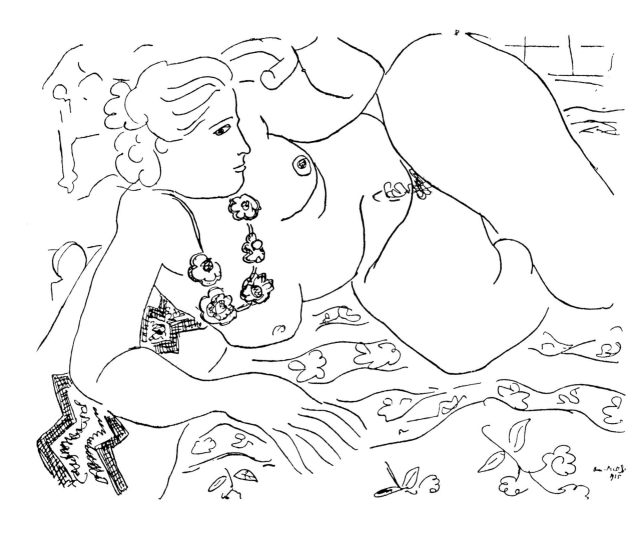

Nude in the Studio, 1935
Pen and ink, 45 x 56 cm
Private collection, USA

but it was not until 1939 that the major theoretical text of his later period, 'A Painter's Notes on Drawing', appeared in print. During the 1930s Matisse mainly produced line drawings done (for the sake of clarity and delicacy) in pencil or ink. Matisse tells us that the ink drawings were done "only after hundreds of preliminary drawings, after try-outs, new insight, new definitions of form. Then I drew with my eyes shut."

'Nude in the Studio' (above) again defies spatial limits, the drawing fills the entire page. The flowing contours expressively create a sensual, feline body, stretched out and posed. The surrounding areas are filled with geometrical and floral patterns, heightening the impact of the woman's body. It is in the nature of line drawing that depth and relief be excluded; on the other hand, the steady, even lines, fluent and apparently undeliberated, create necessary zones and meet Matisse's requirement that "a good drawing must be like a basket from which you cannot remove a single straw without leaving a hole."

The eroticism which we see revived in 'The Dance' was to be a major factor in Matisse's work of the 1930s. The Platonic love that links painter and model was for Matisse a sine qua non of his work: "This relationship is the mutual attachment of things, a shared language – indeed, it is love." Unlike Picasso, Matisse did not see love as being necessarily connected with sexual potency. For him, it was an inward feeling that made a positive view of the world accessible.

Most of his major works of 1935 and 1936 are nudes. In 1936 Lydia Delektorskaya, who also helped with paper cutouts, was the model for his 'Pink Nude' (p. 71), a painting which for all its modesty of scale achieves a sense of the monumental. The woman's arms and legs are bent but still they are trimmed by the edge of the canvas. As in the

"If there is some red spot on one of my paintings it is unlikely to be the heart of the work. The painting was done regardless of it. You could remove the red and still the painting would be there. But in Matisse's work it is inconceivable that you could remove a spot of red, no matter how small, without the entire painting instantly collapsing."
PABLO PICASSO

Pink Nude, 1935
Oil on canvas, 66 x 92.5 cm
Baltimore Museum of Art, Baltimore

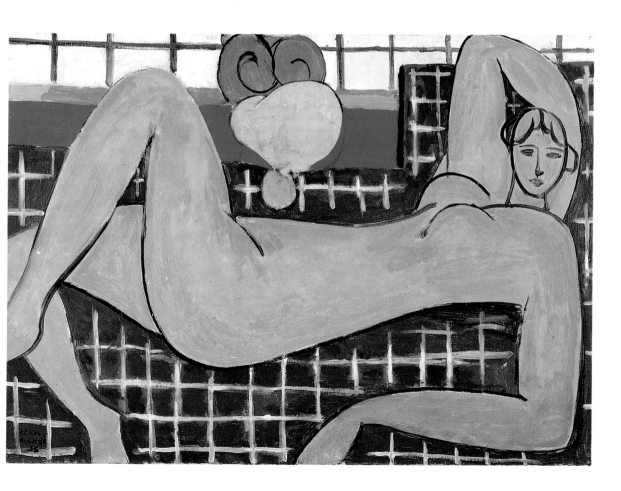

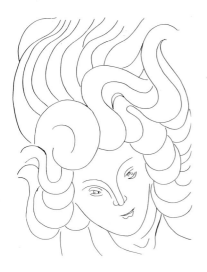

Hair, 1932
Illustration for
Stéphane Mallarmé's 'Poésies'
Etching

Merion 'Dance', the viewer's imagination is urged beyond the spatial limits. The painter has come up to his model as if for a close-up, and the background is a mere setting, with no perspectival depths. The background is no more than a pattern, and the nude a sketch of the human body. What gives the woman her considerable clarity of impact is the emphatic exaggeration of the limbs, the frontal angle of the head, and the suggestion of the two breasts. A balance has been struck between organic and geometric form, smooth and modelled surfaces, curved lines and straight, colours warm and cold, and it is a balance arresting in its simplicity. The paint has a dry, matt texture reminiscent of frescoes on plaster. Matisse himself draws attention to the "beautiful matt quality" of mural painting.

In paintings such as 'Lady in Blue' (right), which followed in the years after 1937, Matisse missed the balance he had achieved. He wrote to fellow-artist Pierre Bonnard: "My drawing is what I need, since it expresses what is distinctive in my own feeling. But my painting is restricted by the new conventions of applying large zones of paint to express myself – nothing but localized colours with neither shadow nor relief, that are supposed to suggest light and spiritual space through their interactions. It doesn't go well with my spontaneity – I relish knocking off some vast work in the space of a minute."

The draughtsmanship of 'Lady in Blue' is of an extreme precision: the fine white lines have been scratched out of the paint, the dark lines drawn with a fine brush or similar implement. These lines define the flat, expansive forms but confer no relief or depth. The woman in the long blue dress with white frills is sitting on an armchair or sofa with curlicued arm-rests like swans' necks. We cannot tell if the black area with criss-cross pattern is the floor or a part of the seat. Nor does the flat arrangement permit any spatial sense. Drawings have been hung on the red rear wall, as if to underline the significance of that medium for this painting. The linear clarity of the painting matches the absence of nuance in the yellow, red, blue, black and white colouring. The use of paint lacks the tension that would establish it on an equal footing with the drawn lines: subordinated, it almost makes an impression of cheerful colourfulness.

Matisse achieved a greater balance of colouring and line drawing in 'Music' (p. 75). In the late Thirties Matisse frequently returned to the subject of two seated women, but what is unusual here is the square format: neither vertical nor horizontal is given preference, and a quiet harmony results. We see a profusion of luxuriant patterns, and two figures with elongated limbs and in attitudes that seem posed for our scrutiny. This painting came after a fireplace decoration on the same subject that Matisse had done for Nelson A. Rockefeller in 1938, though in the earlier work a more stringent solution had been called for.

RIGHT:
Lady in Blue, 1937
Oil on canvas, 93 x 73.6 cm
Mrs. John Wintersteen Collection, Philadelphia

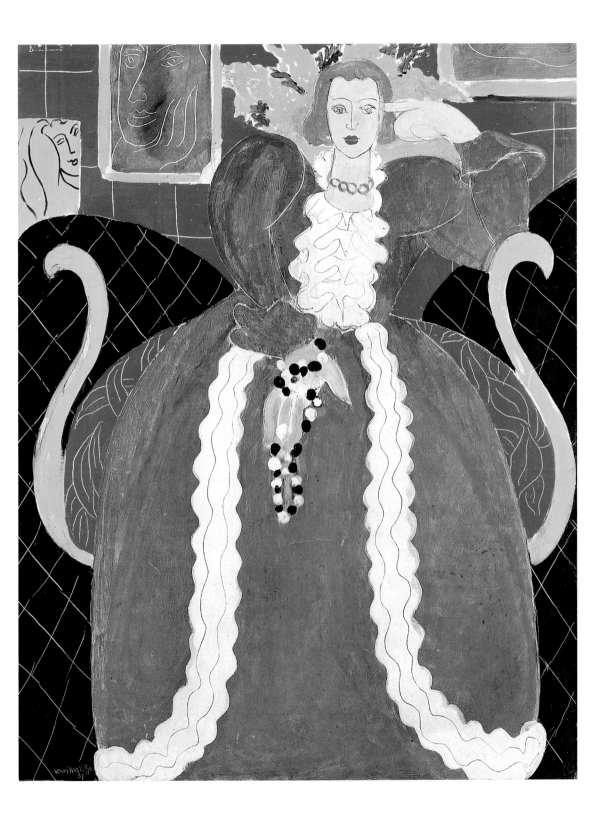

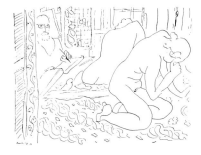

Nude Kneeling in Front of a Mirror, 1937
Pen and ink
Private collection, Paris

In 'Interior with Etruscan Vase' (p. 76), the decorative style has softened into intimacy: the colouring is not so smooth and the forms not so hard. The girl sits reading among the profuse foliage of the plants in the black room, highlighted by the bright window that breaks up the rear wall. On that wall there are drawings, albeit without the programmatic significance they had in the 'Lady in Blue'. Matisse's lines are varied in strength, create a modelled three-dimensionality once again, which is more open and gives the colours the freedom to unfold. As well as pure colours there are mixed, and this helps establish a note of intimacy.

Matisse never forgot that a picture must preserve a sufficient tension among its constituent elements, and in 'Still Life with Oysters' (p. 77) he introduces conflict by turning the table to a diagonal angle. The parallel lines on the tablecloth reinforce the effect of the diagonals. On this base, which conflicts with the rectangle of the canvas, Matisse arranges the components of his still life: napkin, plate, oysters, lemons, green herbs, a jug and a knife. The napkin echoes the diagonal of the tablecloth but its stripes lead in another direction, as does the knife. At the same time, both napkin and knife remain part of the horizontal plane created by the still life. The diagonal position of the tabletop implies a total image that goes beyond the confines of the canvas.

We feel the same tendency to expand the pictorial space in 'The Rumanian Blouse' (p. 66). We see a woman three quarters turned to us; but her head is cut by the upper edge of the picture, and the centrifugal force that seems to inform the lines of her white blouse thrusts far beyond the limits of the painting. The patterning of the blouse lacks a focal point, the centre of the picture remains empty. How much more important, then, above this ballooning blouse, the woman's bud-like head becomes! Though the colour gleams it remains as flat as the drawing: but what distinguishes the two elements is that the lines move expansively out while the colours have a confining effect. During 1940, Matisse took an embroidered Rumanian blouse as the central motif in other similar paintings, 'The Dream' and 'Sleeping Woman'. What all these paintings share is an emotional expressiveness that recalls certain madonnas of the early Italian Renaissance.

Such paintings have an unforced, natural quality, and a harmonic, inevitable simplicity; yet they were the product of long, hard work. It took Matisse a full year to complete 'The Dream' (p. 2). The woman is wrapped in her costume – the Rumanian blouse – as if in some arabesque, near-abstract design in which her head and hands are resting. The three wavy lines that represent her hair might just as well be taken as part of the pattern of the blouse. Her right arm, unnaturally elongated, expresses a wrapped, embracing security, and so symbolizes the tranquil relaxation of sleep. There is tension, it is

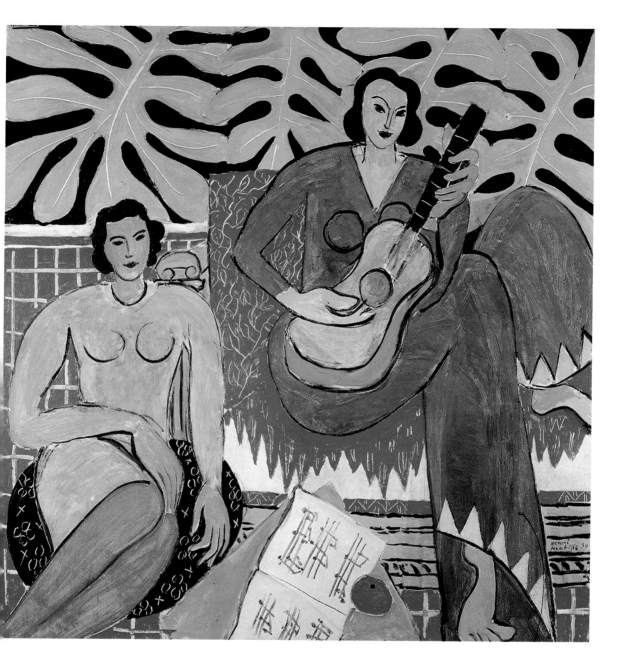

Music, 1939
Oil on canvas, 115 x 115 cm
Albright-Knox Art Gallery, Buffalo

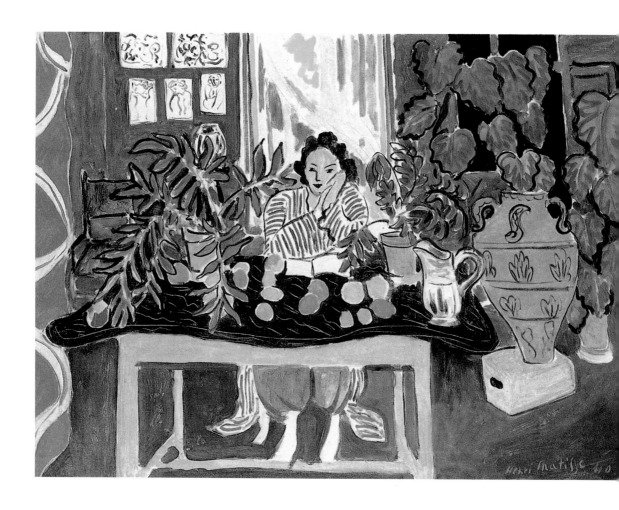

Interior with Etruscan Vase, 1940
Oil on canvas, 73.6 x 108 cm
Cleveland Museum of Art, Cleveland

true, in the ochre, pink, violet and red colouring, and the various planes; but they do not diminish the effect of peacefulness.

Matisse was beset with worries in the Second World War, but his art remained one of tranquil and consolatory power. In May 1940 German troops marched into France, and Matisse, though he had a visa valid for Brazil, decided to remain. From Nice he wrote to his son Pierre, who was running a gallery in New York: "Perhaps I would feel better, freer, less downcast elsewhere. But when I was at the frontier and saw the endless stream of people departing, I wasn't thinking of escape at all, though I had my passport in my pocket complete with Brazilian visa. I was to have gone to Rio de Janeiro on 8th June, via Modane and Genoa, to spend a month there – but when I saw events had taken a turn for the worse I had them return the fare for my ticket. I would have felt like a deserter. If everyone of any value left, what would remain of France?"

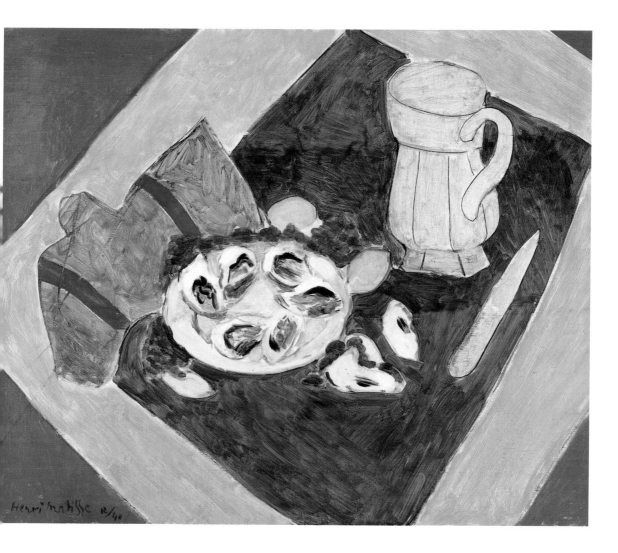

Still Life with Oysters, 1940
Oil on canvas, 65.5 x 81.5 cm
Kunstmuseum, Basle

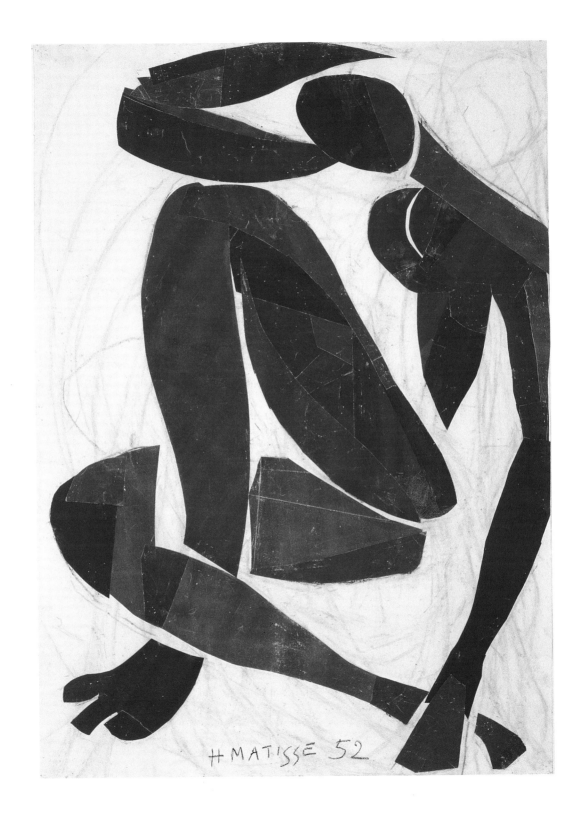

Matisse's Second Life: an Art of Grace 1941-1954

A "second life" was vouchsafed Henri Matisse in 1941. His intestinal troubles had grown worse and he was unable to work in peace. Camoin and his daughter Marguerite prompted him to undergo treatment, and Matisse transferred to Lyon, where Professor Leriche operated on him. He was in hospital for nearly three months, and afterwards came down with flu for another two. It was a minor miracle that he survived an operation for duodenal cancer plus the two pulmonary embolisms that followed.

Matisse returned to the Hotel Regina, high up at Cimiez, where he had been living since the end of 1938 on the orders of his doctor, who had advised against sea air. After an air raid on Cimiez, he moved to 'Le Rêve', a villa at Vence. In the years from 1941 to 1944, Matisse was often bedridden. He had a prolapsed stomach and had to wear an iron belt that made it impossible for him to remain standing for any long stretch. No doubt it was this state of health that resulted in the small scale of his work at that time, much of it book illustrations. In illustrating Pierre de Ronsard's 'Florilège des Amours', Henry de Montherlant's 'Pasiphaé' or Charles d'Orléans's 'Poèmes', Matisse was always concerned to establish an equilibrium of printing and illustrated page.

Since 1939, Matisse had been visiting the Greek publisher Emmanuel Tériade, who edited the magazine 'Verve'. In the editorial offices, Matisse would make cut-outs from catalogues of printer's inks, and some of these cut-outs were used for the cover of issue VIII of the magazine. Tériade was keen to publish an entire book of them, but it was not until 1943 that the artist agreed. The following year the twenty pictures were already finished for the book, which was to be titled 'Jazz'. The printers' ink had been abandoned, and replaced with gouache which was applied to sheets which were then used for the cut-outs. It was difficult to find a satisfactory way of reproducing the pictures, so the book did not appear until 1947.

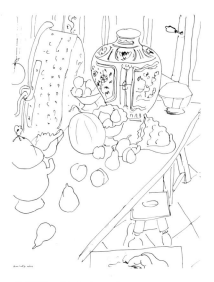

Still Life with Fruits and Chinese Vase, 1941
Pen and ink, 52 x 40 cm
Musée National d'Art Moderne,
Centre Georges Pompidou, Paris

LEFT:
Blue Nude IV, 1952
Gouache on paper cut-out, 103 x 74 cm
Musée Henri Matisse, Nice

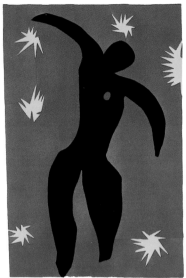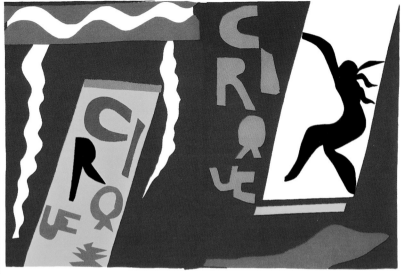

ABOVE LEFT:
Icarus, 1947
Illustration for the book 'Jazz',
screen-print after
gouache on paper cut-out

ABOVE RIGHT:
The Circus, 1947
Illustration for the book 'Jazz',
screen-print after
gouache on paper cut-out

"Cutting straight into colour reminds me of what a
sculptor does to his stone. This is the spirit in
which this book was conceived ... These pictures
in lively and powerful colours arose out of crystal-
lized recollections of the circus, folk-tales or
travels."   HENRI MATISSE

The title 'Jazz' is best understood if we see it not in relation to the
contents but to the manner of presentation. Matisse explained: "True
jazz has a number of excellent qualities: the gift of improvization, of
life, of harmony with the listening audience." The book approaches
naive, spontaneous folk-art, drawing its inspiration from folk tales,
circus performances, and travel. The pictures of circus life usually
consist of angular shapes while the 'Lagoons' are flowing and
rounded. The book covers the range from the stars of 'Icarus' to algae.

The small-format experience of working on 'Jazz' offered Matisse
visual solutions to various problems, and he took his new principles
further in 'Polynesia, The Sky' and 'Polynesia, The Sea' (right). These
cut-outs came into being in 1946 as designs for tapestries to be woven
at the Gobelin looms of Beauvais. On a ground of pale and darker blue
rectangles we see a number of shapes – ambiguous, arabesque,
curved, all of them white. Sky and sea overlap. Plants, fish and birds
exist side by side.

The relaxed serenity of Matisse's visual world is the more
remarkable if we remember that the war years brought him his share
of troubles too. In 1944, with astonishing calm, he wrote to Marquet:
"My family are all in the best of health. Today I received a telegram
from New York – my children and grandchildren are well. In April,
though, Madame Matisse and Marguerite were arrested by the
Gestapo. Madame Matisse was in prison at Fresnes for three months
and then was given another three-month sentence. This she bore
courageously. Marguerite was in solitary confinement in Rennes till

August and was then moved to Belfort, and now, after some weeks in the mountains, she is back in Paris."

Matisse's health improved enough for him to resume painting in oils. In 1944 the Argentinian diplomat Enchorrena, who was resident in Paris, commissioned a door to connect his bedroom and bathroom. Initially Matisse opted to present an idyllic theme: a nymph sleeping, observed by a faun. But both subject and composition left the artist dissatisfied, and his work was a trial to him and stagnated. The diplomat persisted, and Matisse tried again. He chose a new subject, and this time succeeded. The mythological 'Leda and the Swan' (p. 82) has been stripped of all narrative content. Jupiter, who according to the myth came to Leda in the form of a swan, can be seen in the upper part of the picture, his arabesquely curved neck and head bending across a black space to Leda, who turns away. The monumental female nude has been fashioned sparingly and vastly. The emphatic, streamlined figure has something heroic, and restores the dignity to the myth. To right and left, red panels with a leaf design provide the triptych's frame and give Matisse's interpretation a revelatory flavour.

"Colour is a means of expressing light, though not so much light as a physical phenomenon as the light that exists in reality – in the artist's head."
HENRI MATISSE

Polynesia, The Sea, 1946
Gouache on paper cut-out, 200 x 314 cm
Musée National d'Art Moderne,
Centre Georges Pompidou, Paris

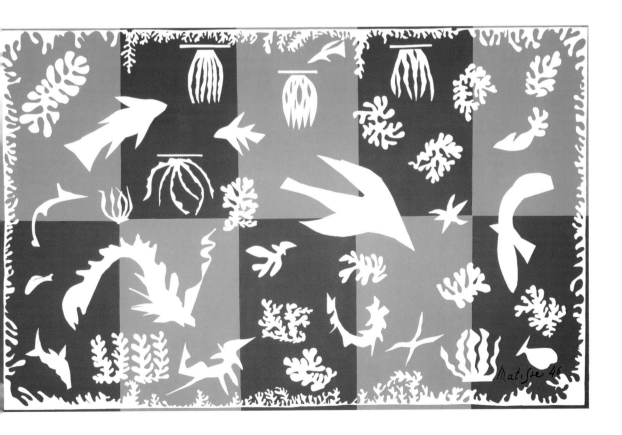

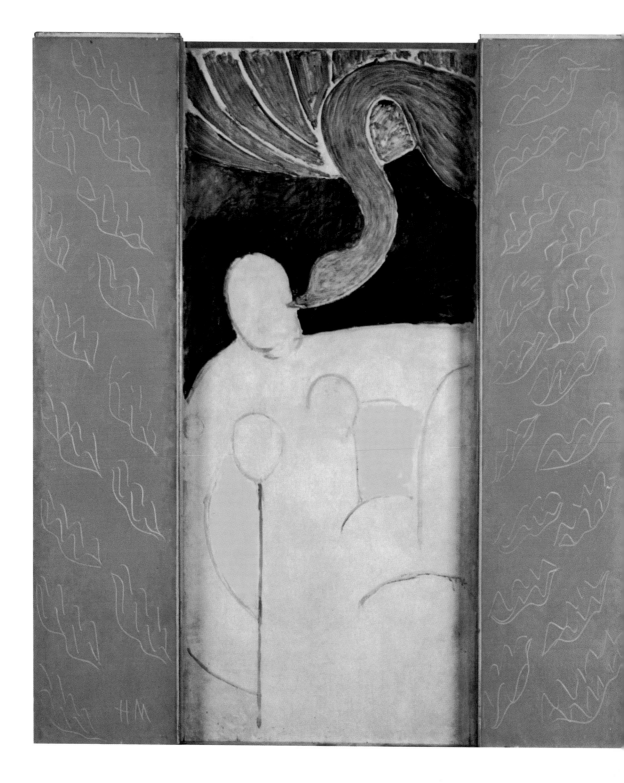

Between 1946 and 1948, Matisse painted a number of interiors where his colours again touched a height of intensity: 'Red Interior, Still Life on a Blue Table', 'Large Red Interior' and 'The Egyptian Curtain'. All of them share a love of contrast: inside and out, bright and dark, still life and landscape, straight lines and curved, the spartan and the copious. As if it were wholly unproblematic, Matisse manages to present all his pictorial elements at the same level: in doing so, he achieves the absolute equivalence of line and colour.

In the 'Red Interior, Still Life on a Blue Table' (p. 84) the motif, as in the other interiors, is almost everyday, with nothing unusual to attract our attention. It shows a room with a medallion on the wall. A round table, with fruits and a vase of flowers, stands near the open verandah door, through which we can see into the garden. The picture's powerful impact derives from its décor and colourfulness. The artist has shrewdly kept to a very few tones of yellow, red, blue and green – Matisse, after all, held that "an avalanche of colours loses all its force. Colour can achieve its full expressive power only if it is organized, and its degree of intensity corresponds to the emotion in the artist." This correspondence appears inevitable in this interior. A black zigzag has been introduced to the red walls and floor, enlivening the surfaces and enhancing the spatial depth of the picture. The black lines render the red equivalent to the other colours. The spatial qualities of the picture are easy to grasp, but what prevails is colour, arranged in zones, and the objects seem somehow dematerialized. It is as if Matisse had applied principles learnt in the composition of cut-outs to his paintings. This interior is a work radiant with harmony and undiluted joie de vivre.

If we turn to the 'Large Red Interior' (p. 85) we find a painting and a drawing in Indian ink on the wall, both of them interiors, as if to say that the two media are of equal value. Colours and lines modulate with unforced ease across the red ground of the picture. Matisse's late paintings were accompanied by ink drawings on the same subjects.

'The Egyptian Curtain' (p. 86) is considered the artist's last major painting. In it, Matisse again turns to an old favourite theme, the window. Beyond the window, a palm is exploding in a firework of leafage; beneath the window the painter has placed another favourite motif, a still life of fruits. His enthusiasm for materials with striking patterns, such as in this Egyptian curtain, had provided the title for this painting. In this work as in others before, black is conspicuously deployed, not to express darkness but to reflect light. The brightness of the other colours becomes all the more intense. The canvas itself can be made out through thin paint at points, and elsewhere has been left unpainted, so that it too contributes to the overall image. 'The Egyptian Curtain' achieves a constant interchange of positives and negatives, and so creates an effortless meshing of spatial depth and decorative surface.

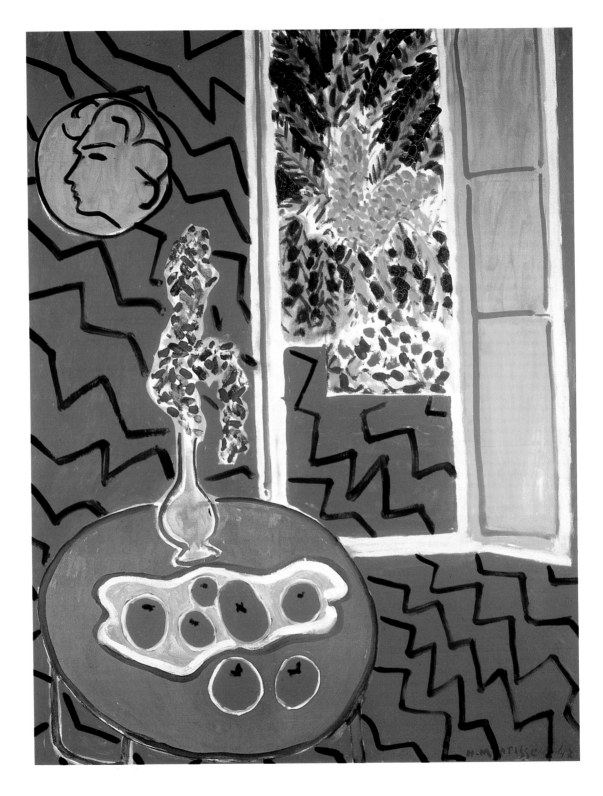

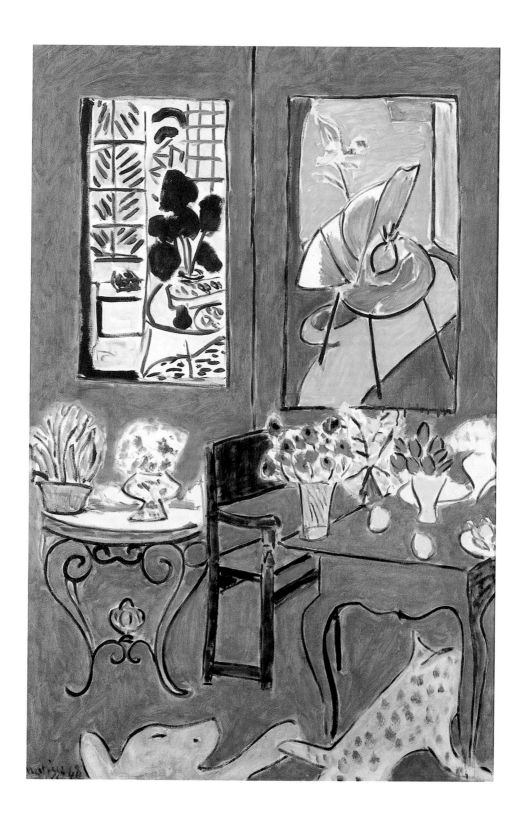

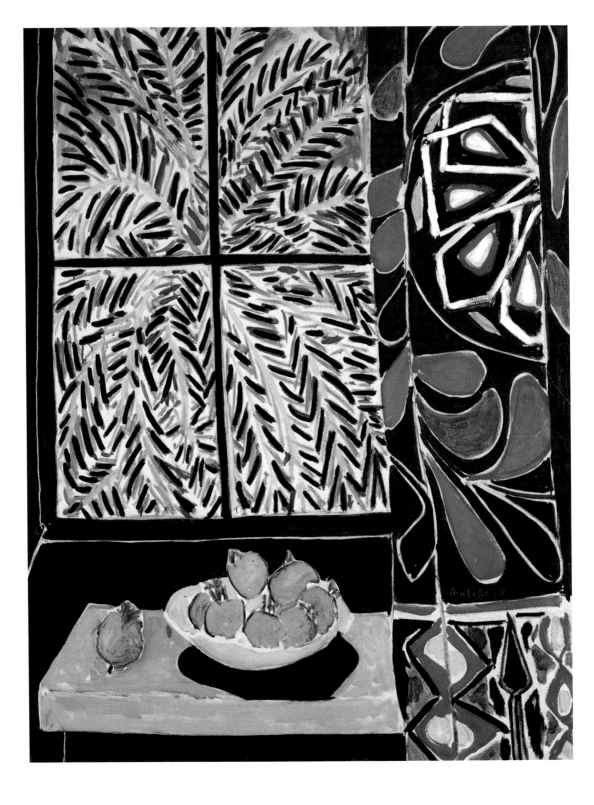

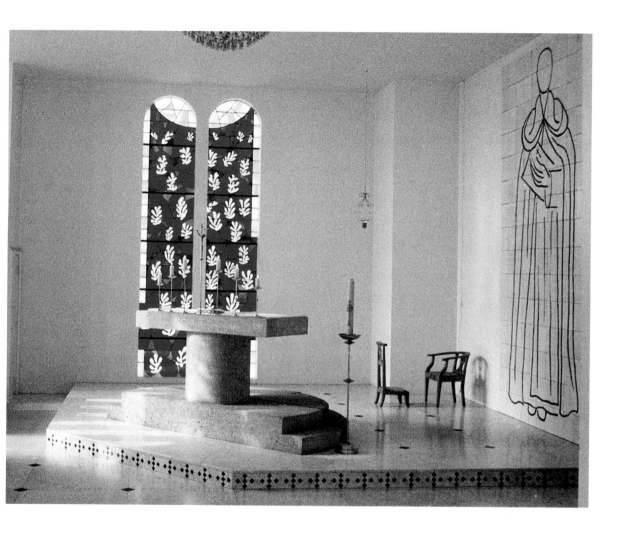

For several years, Matisse was kept occupied by one single project, the Chapel of the Rosary in Vence (above). He had accepted the commission out of friendship for Miss Monique Bougeois, who had been his nurse in Nice during 1942/43. She had subsequently helped with the paper cut-outs for 'Jazz'. In 1946, as Sister Jacques-Marie, she moved to the Dominican Foyer Lacordaire at Vence, where she was able to resume contact with Matisse. When she had the idea of stained glass windows for the shed which served as the nuns' chapel, she naturally consulted Matisse. Her enthusiasm was infectious, and soon Matisse had decided to do the stained glass himself, as well as designing the building to house them. Matisse could see from the outset that light was the most important factor. Through the Stations of the Cross and the stained glass he would create a contrast of line drawing and colour: he proposed drawing the

Interior of the Chapel of the Rosary, Vence, 1950
At left: The Tree of Life, stained glass
At right: St. Dominic, ceramic tiles

LEFT:
The Egyptian Curtain, 1948
Oil on canvas, 116.2 x 88.9 cm
Phillips Collection, Washington

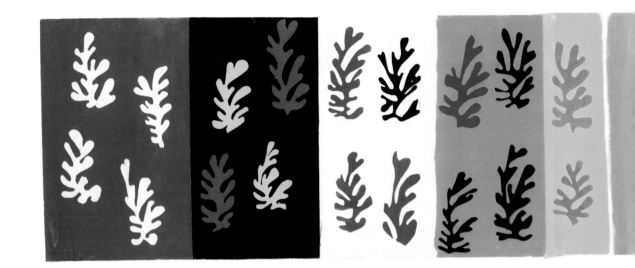

Stations on terracotta, while with regard to the stained glass he remarked, leafing through 'Jazz': "These are the colours of stained glass. I cut out these gouache sheets just as you would cut glass – with the difference that they need to reflect the light, whereas glass needs to let it through."

Matisse became deeply involved in his labours for the chapel, and was able to see them through to completion. His designs were made with paper cut-outs. After some discussion, a subject was agreed, a passage from the Revelation of St. John (22:2): "In the midst of the street of it, and on either side of the river, was there the tree of life, which bare twelve manner of fruits, and yielded her fruit every month: and the leaves of the tree were for the healing of the nations." The tree of life represents the coming Golden Age. The glasswork consists of long thin strips topped with semicircles. The areas of wall space between the windows have the effect of a colonnade. The leaves of the tree of life are arranged so that they appear to reach out from the wall spaces, and these spaces themselves take on the role of stems. The flowers, touching now at the top and now at the bottom, settle into continuous waves, some yellow, some blue. Waves are symbolic of eternity. At the window by the altar we find philodendron shapes in radiant yellow on a ground of blue and green. The motif of the tree of life does not occupy the entire space, but instead retreats in a semicircular shape from the rounded arches, as if the pattern were in

"In the chapel my main task was to create an equilibrium between one surface that was filled with light and colour and opposite wall which was relieved only by line drawings in black on white. For me, the chapel meant the fulfilment of a whole life devoted to my work. It was the flowering of hard and difficult but honest labours."

HENRI MATISSE

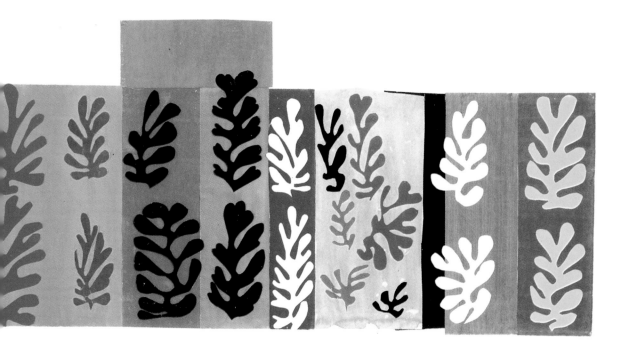

fact on some cloth hung up and fastened at the corners. The stained glass gives the impression of being material hung in front of the windows.

The remaining walls are decorated in a script-like black and white. Three areas of ceramic tiles, consisting of white enamelled tiles with black line drawings done in brush, show the Stations of the Cross, the Virgin with Child, and St. Dominic. The representations are stripped to a bare minimum of signs. Mary appears like a flower, amid a floral design. The word AVE has been added. St. Dominic, founder of the order, wears vestments that fall into stiff folds, and has something of a tree-trunk, with the arm holding the book growing out like a branch. Both Mary and St. Dominic are fairly static in presentation, but the Stations are marked by considerable dynamism. This series of images gave Matisse his greatest problems, since the content conflicted deeply with his own view of life. In the end, after Matisse had worked on it for four years, the chapel was consecrated on 25th June, 1951, by the Bishop of Nice. It was work of considerable importance in Matisse's development. For him, it represented "the image of a great open book".

The debate whether art should be representational or not, which raged in the years following the Second World War, occupied Matisse somewhat when he visited Paris. He was aware that he had little time left to finish his life's work and was wary of any upheaval, but at the

Composition (The Velvets), 1947
Gouache on paper cut-out, 51.5 x 217 cm
Kunstmuseum, Basle

"You have to know how to preserve that freshness and innocence a child has when it approaches things. You have to remain a child your whole life long and yet be a man who draws his energy from the things of the world."   HENRI MATISSE

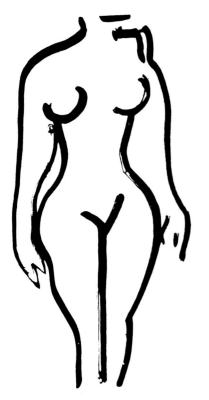

Large Nude, 1951
Brush and ink

Zulma, 1950
Gouache on paper cut-out, 238 x 130 cm
Statens Museum for Kunst, Copenhagen

same time he was sensitive to the abstraction that was then prevalent. In 1947 he wrote: "Since I returned from Paris I have been undergoing a kind of crisis, and I do not think it impossible that I shall find my art taking a significantly new direction. I sense a need to be free of all compulsion and all theoretical ideas, to express myself fully, beyond this fashionable distinction between the representational and the non-representational." Matisse hit upon a synthesis that might well serve to describe his late work: "Abstraction rooted in reality".

Three years remained to him after the consecration of the Chapel of the Rosary. He worked hard, in more absolute, abstract terms. The lined-up rectangular basic form of 'Composition (The Velvets)' (pp. 88/89) is derived from 'Polynesia, The Sea': the rigidity of the grid is dissolved, the relation of forms and background relaxed. In the 'Polynesia' work, the plant and animal motifs take charge, proclaiming that the organic is master of the mechanical. The distinct levels of figure and background are no longer separate. In the case of human figures, the distinction survives more doggedly: 'Zulma' (right) is constructed like a painting, and retains a sense of perspective. 'Blue Nude IV' (p. 78), shaped against a white ground, also has a scrupulous sense of the spatial position of the limbs. The effect of Matisse's blue nudes is of sculpture done in some intangible material. They have a sculptural physicality, yet at the same time a flat, decorative precision. And they are wholly removed from any environment. These cut-outs took Matisse weeks of trial and error before he found satisfactory positions: and in the cut-outs using plant motifs his conception of the decorative in art is triumphantly vindicated.

Matisse's last work, the Rockefeller 'Rose', is stiff and stylized and reflects the artist's exhaustion. On 15th October, 1954, he had the model for this rose, which was intended for Mrs. Nelson Rockefeller's chapel, laid out on his floor, and he continued working at it till his death. On 3rd November, 1954, Henri Matisse died of a heart attack.

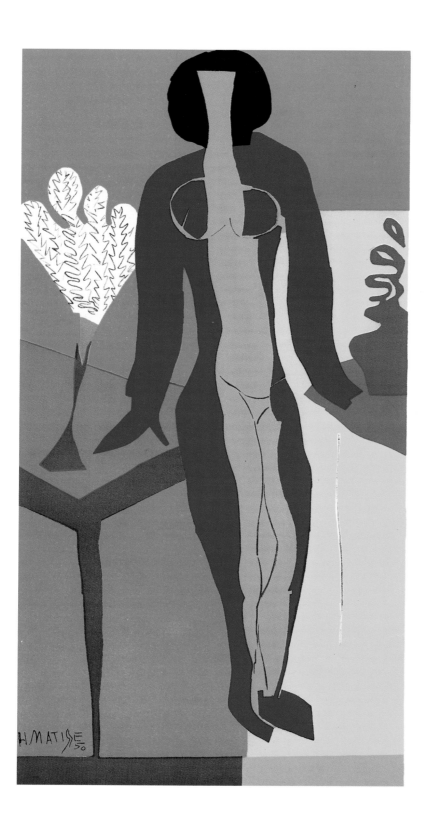

Henri Matisse 1869-1954:
A Chronology

1869   Henri-Emile-Benoit Matisse is born on 31st December at Le Cateau-Cambrésis in northern France at his grandparents' farm. His parents, Emile Matisse and Héloise Gérard, have a general store selling household goods and seed at Bohain-en-Vermandois (Aisne). Henri grows up at Bohain.

1872   Birth of his brother Emile-Auguste.

1882-1887   Henri attends the grammar school at Saint-Quentin.

1887/88   Studies law in Paris, passing his diploma.

1889   Works in Saint-Quentin as a lawyer's assistant. In the early mornings he attends a drawing course at the Ecole Quentin de la Tour.

1890   Confined to his bed for nearly a year following an intestinal operation. Takes up drawing as a pastime.

1891   Abandons his legal career to become a painter. He matriculates at the Académie Julian in Paris, and prepares for the Ecole des Beaux-Arts entrance examination.

1892   Leaves the Académie Julian, and goes to evening classes at the Ecole des Arts Décoratifs. Friendship with Marquet begins. Copies works by Poussin, Raphael, Chardin, David and others in the Louvre.

1893   Works unofficially in Moreau's studio at the Ecole des Beaux-Arts. Meets Rouault, Camoin and Manguin there.

1894   Birth of his daughter Marguerite. Matisse does not marry the mother, Amélie Parayre, till 1898.

1895   Resident in the Quai Saint-Michel. Officially a student of Moreau's at the Ecole des Beaux-Arts. He begins to paint out of doors. Visit to Britanny in the summer. Copies numerous works in the Louvre.

1896   Exhibits four paintings at the Salon de la Société Nationale, selling two

Matisse at work on 'Still Life with "La Danse" (p. 32) in his studio at Issy-les-Moulineaux, 1909

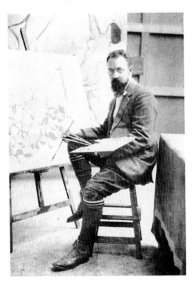

Self-portrait, 1906
Oil on canvas, 55 x 46 cm
Statens Museum for Kunst, Copenhagen

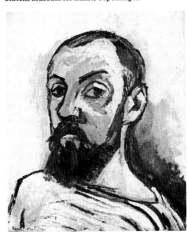

Hans Purrmann, Albert Weisgerber and Henri Matisse (left to right) at the Munich Löwenbräu, 1910

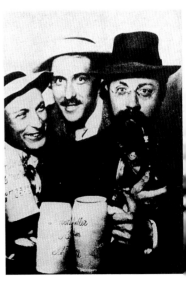

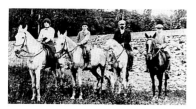

Matisse out riding with his children
Marguerite, Pierre and Jean (left to right)
at Clamart near Paris, around 1910

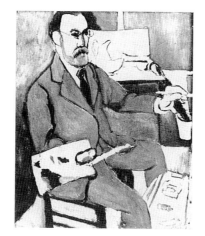

Self-portrait, 1918
Oil on canvas, 65 x 54 cm
Musée Henri Matisse, Le Cateau

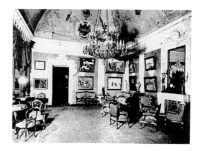

Sergei Shchukin's Matisse room in Moscow.
The Russian collector, who commissioned 'La Danse'
(pp. 30/31) and 'La Musique' (p. 29) and other
paintings, owned 37 important works by Matisse,
only ten of which can be seen in this photograph.

of them. In Britanny during the summer he meets the painter Russel, who shows him Van Gogh's work.

1897 Discovers the Impressionists at the Musée du Luxembourg. Further visit to Britanny. Exhibits 'Dinner Table' (p. 8) and is met with criticism.

1898 Marries Amélie Parayre from Toulouse. Honeymoon in London, where on Pissarro's advice Matisse studies the paintings of Turner. Six months on Corsica, then to Toulouse and Fenouillet.

1899 After the death of Moreau, Matisse quits the Ecole des Beaux-Arts on account of disagreements with Moreau's successor Cormon. Birth of son Jean. Studies at the Académie Carrière with Derain. Evening classes in sculpture. Painting out of doors in the Jardin du Luxembourg, Arcueil, and at the Quai Saint-Michel, with Marquet. Buys a Cézanne from Vollard.

1900 Birth of son Pierre. Financial difficulties. With Marquet, Matisse paints the decorations for the Grand Palais, for the Great Exhibition. His wife opens a boutique.

1901 Recuperates from bronchitis in Switzerland. Exhibits at the Salon des Indépendants, which Signac presides over. At a Van Gogh exhibition, Derain introduces him to Vlaminck.

1902 Financial problems oblige him to spend the winter with his parents at Bohain. Together with former students of Moreau he exhibits at Berthe Weill's gallery in Paris.

1903 Exhibits at the autumn salon (the first of its kind) with friends, among them Rouault and Derain. Visits an exhibition of Islamic art. First etchings.

1904 First solo show at Vollard's gallery. In the summer he meets Signac at St. Tropez. Attempts at a neo-Impressionist technique. Thirteen pictures in the autumn salon.

1905 Signac buys 'Luxe, calme et volupté' (p. 10). Spends the summer at Collioure with Derain, and sees the paintings of Gauguin. Exhibits at the autumn salon, together with Derain, Marquet, Vlaminck, Rouault and others, and sparks off a controversy. The group is ironically nicknamed 'Les Fauves' (the wild ones). 'Woman with the Hat' (p. 15) prompts a scandal, and is bought by the Steins. Matisse hires a studio in the Rue Sèvres. Paints 'Madame Matisse, "The Green Line"' (p. 16).

1906 Leo Stein buys 'La Joie de Vivre' (p. 20). Travels to Biskra in Algeria (cf. p. 21) and is fascinated by ceramics and cloths there. Summer at Collioure. Meets Picasso at the Steins' house and shows him an African sculpture. First lithographs and woodcuts.

1907 Visits Padua, Florence, Arezzo and Siena. Picasso and Matisse exchange paintings. Exhibits 'Luxe, I' (p. 25) at autumn salon. Admirers, among them Sarah Stein and the painters Purrmann and Moll, found a school where Matisse instructs.

1908 Transfers school to Boulevard des Invalides. Trip to Bavaria in summer. First exhibitions in New York, Moscow and Berlin. Paints 'Harmony in Red' (p. 27).

1909 The Moscow businessman Shchukin commissions 'La Danse' (pp. 30/31) and 'La Musique' (p. 29). Summer at Cavalière. Leaves Paris and buys a house at Issy-les-Moulineaux, where he builds a studio. Visit to Berlin.

1910 Major retrospective at the Bernheim-Jeune Gallery in Paris. 'La Danse' and 'La Musique' are shown at the autumn salon. Travels to Munich with Marquet, and sees Islamic exhibition. Particularly impressed by carpets. Journey to Spain in the autumn.

1911 Painting in Seville, Issy and Collioure. In November travels to Moscow and sees Shchukin; studies icons. Spends the winter in Morocco.

1912 Winter in Morocco. Spring in Issy. The Russian collector Morozov buys his first pictures. In the winter Matisse makes a second Moroccan journey, to Tangier, with Marquet.

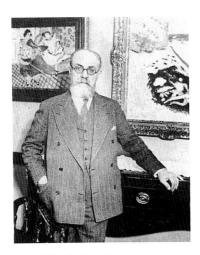

Matisse in Etta Cone's apartment
in Baltimore, December 1930

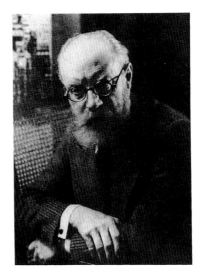

Henri Matisse in 1930

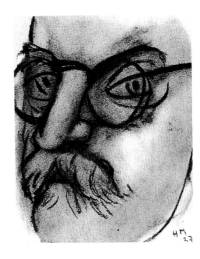

1913   Return from Tangier in spring.
Moroccan pictures exhibited in Paris.
Exhibits in the Armory Show in New York
and the Secession in Berlin. Summer at
Issy. In the autumn Matisse again moves
to the studio on the Quai Saint-Michel in
Paris.

1914   Exhibition in Berlin: the pictures
are confiscated when the war breaks out.
Matisse is not called up for military
service, though he requests it. Spends
summer with his family and Marquet at
Collioure. Gets to know Juan Gris. Paints
'View of Notre-Dame' (p. 45) and 'French
Window at Collioure' (p. 47).

1915   Exhibition in New York. Painting
at Paris and Issy. Paints the Italian model
Laurette (pp. 52/53). Visits Arcachon near
Bordeaux.

1916   Painting in Paris and Issy. Spends
a first winter in Nice at the Hotel
Beau-Rivage.

1917   Summer at Issy, autumn in Paris,
winter in Nice. Visits Renoir at Cagnes.

1918   Joint show with Picasso. Rents a
villa in Nice. Summer at Cherbourg and
Paris. In the autumn he returns to Nice.
Visits Bonnard at Antibes and Renoir at
Cagnes.

1919   Exhibitions in Paris and London.
Summer at Issy. Paints 'The Black Table'
(p. 61) using Antoinette as model.

1920   Designs the set and costumes for
Stravinsky's ballet 'The Nightingale'.
Accompanies the Russian ballet to
London. Summer at Etretat.

1921   Summer at Etretat. Autumn in
Nice, where he rents an apartment.
Divides his time between Paris and Nice.

1922   Paints his series of odalisques
and begins a series of lithographs.

Self-portrait, 1937
Charcoal on paper, 25.5 x 20.5 cm
Private collection

Matisse at work on 'Nymph in the Forest'
(Musée Matisse, Nice), around 1936

1923   The Shchukin and Morozov
collections form the basis of the first
museum of modern western art in
Moscow (now known at the Pushkin
Museum), including 48 pictures by
Matisse.

1924   Important retrospective in
Copenhagen.

1925   Second journey to Italy, with his
wife and daughter. Paints 'Decorative
Figure on an Ornamental Background' (p.
50).

1927   Pierre Matisse organizes a show
in New York. Matisse receives the
painting prize of the Carnegie Internatio-
nal Exhibition in Pittsburgh.

1930   Travels to New York, San
Francisco and Tahiti. Visits the Barnes
Foundation at Merion and is com-
missioned to make a mural.

1931 – 1933   Major retrospective in
Berlin, Paris, Basle and New York.
Working on 'The Dance' (pp. 68/69) for the
Barnes Foundation. Etchings to illustrate
Mallarmé's 'Poésie'. Travels to Merion to
instal 'The Dance'. Holidays in Venice and
Padua.

1934/35   From this period, further
exhibitions in his son Pierre's gallery in
New York. Etchings to illustrate James
Joyce's 'Ulysses'. Lydia Delektorskaya,
later to be his secretary, models for the

'Pink Nude' (p. 71). Cardboard designs for carpets.

1936/37 Donates his Cézanne to the Museum of Paris. Set and costumes for a Shostakovich ballet, for the Russian ballet. At the Exposition des Mâitres de l'art indépendant in the Petit Palais, an entire room is devoted to Matisse. Paints the 'Lady in Blue' (p. 73).

1938 Moves into an apartment in what was formerly the Hotel Regina at Cimiez near Nice, which he keeps until his death.

1939 Paints 'Music' (p. 75). During the summer works in the Hotel Lutétia in Paris. Leaves Paris on the outbreak of war and returns to Nice.

1940 Spring in Paris, in the Boulevard du Montparnasse. Obtains a visa for Brazil but stays in France. Travels via Bordeaux, Ciboure, Carcassonne and Marseilles to Nice. Separation from Amélie. Paints 'The Rumanian Blouse' (p. 66) and 'The Dream' (p. 2).

1941 Undergoes surgery for duodenal cancer in January at Lyon. Pulls through and returns to work with new verve. Returns to Nice in May. Often works in bed or wheelchair.

1942 Aragon visits at Cimiez. Works on book illustrations. Exchanges paintings with Picasso.

1943 After an air raid on Cimiez he

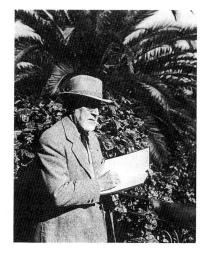

Matisse at Vence in 1946

moves into the 'Le Rêve' villa at Vence (where he stays until 1948). In spite of ill health he goes on working. Begins gouache cut-outs for 'Jazz' (p. 80).

1944 Madame Matisse is arrested. His daughter Marguerite is taken away, charged with Résistance activities.

1945 Returns to Paris in summer. Major show in the hall of honour at the autumn salon. Joint exhibition with Picasso in London.

1946/47 Carpet designs. Film on Matisse at work. Book illustrations. 'Jazz'

is published. Matisse is made a commander of the legion of honour. The Musée National d'Art Moderne begins its Matisse collection. Matisse starts work on the Chapel of the Rosary at Vence.

1948 First major cut-outs. The series of interiors (pp. 84-86) marks a temporary stop in his painting career. Retrospective in Philadelphia.

1949/50 Return to Cimiez. The foundation stone is laid in Vence. The Vence designs are exhibited in Paris. Matisse is awarded the Grand Prize of the Venice Biennale. 'Zulma' (p. 91).

1951 Asthma and angina pectoris. Continues work on the chapel at Vence, which is consecrated in June (p. 87). Retrospective in Museum of Modern Art, New York. Work on cut-outs.

1952 Matisse Museum at Le Cateau opened. Series of blue nudes (p. 78).

1953 Exhibits cut-outs in Paris, sculptures in London.

1954 Dies on 3rd November and is buried in the cemetery at Cimiez.

Working on a plaster model, around 1953/54

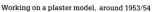

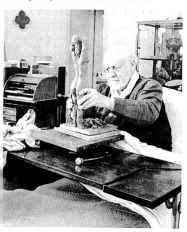

In the Hotel Regina at Cimiez near Nice, 1949

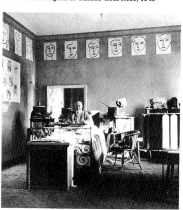

One of the last photographs of Matisse

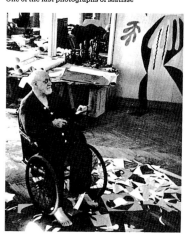

The author and publisher wish to thank the estate of Matisse, in particular
Wanda de Guébriant and Georges Matisse, who helped to make the best colour
reproductions of Matisse's works, the museums, collectors, photographers and archives
who gave permission for the reproduction of works on the following pages:
Archiv für Kunst und Geschichte, Berlin (57); Artothek, Peissenberg (37, 41, 53, 77);
The Bridgeman Art Library, London (11, 20, 35, 49, 59, 62/63, 84, 85, 87);
Fondation Beyeler, Basle (55);Les Héritiers Matisse (17, 27, 40, 47);
Réunion des Musées Nationaux, Paris (43, 81); Ville de Nice (78);
Publisher's archive for all further illustrations.
Particular thanks are due to Benteli Verlag in Berne, the Zurich Kunsthaus and
the Düsseldorf Kunsthalle, for their support.
The author would like to acknowledge his indebtedness to Pierre Schneider's authoritative
study of Matisse (London, 1984). Translations of Matisse's own words in the main and
marginal texts of this book have been newly made for this edition.
We should also like to thank the following for their support: Gilles Néret, Paris; Hélène
Adant; André Held, Eclubens; Ingo F. Walther, Alling; Walther & Walther Verlag, Alling.